...AND A STAR IS BORN

ICONIC CAPSULE OF INSPIRATION FROM THOSE WHO LIVE IN YOUR HEART

...AND A STAR IS BORN

ICONIC CAPSULE OF INSPIRATION FROM THOSE WHO LIVE IN YOUR HEART

DINESH VERMA

- *The inspiring Journey of the Celluloid Actors.*
- *21 Signature teachings to directly implement, to meet the star in you.*

Published Internationally by

Pendown Press

Powered by Gullybaba.com

PENDOWN PRESS
Powered by **Gullybaba Publishing House Pvt. Ltd.,**
An ISO 9001 & ISO 14001 certified Co.,
Regd. Office: 2525/193, 1st Floor, Onkar Nagar-A, Tri Nagar, Delhi-110035, (From Kanhaiya Nagar Metro Station Towards Old Bus Stand)
Branch Office: 1A/2A, 20, Hari Sadan, Ansari Road, Daryaganj, New Delhi-110002
Ph.: 09350849407, 011-27387998
E-mail: info@pendownpress.com
Website: PendownPress.com

New Edition: 2020

ISBN: 978-93-81638-99-6

Contents

Dedication...vii

Few Words ix

Introduction xi

Acknowledgements xiii

1. Amitabh Bachchan 1

2. Dilip Kumar 7

3. Akshay Kumar 13

4. Aamir Khan 19

5. Salman Khan 27

6. Shah Rukh Khan 33

7. Raj Kapoor 41

8. Mohammad Rafi 47

9. Asha Bhosle 53

10. Rajesh Khanna 61

11. A. R. Rahman 67

12. Rajinikanth 73

13. Madhuri Dixit 79

14. Sanjay Dutt 85

15. Hrithik Roshan 91

16. Amrish Puri 97

17. Anil Kapoor 103

18. Govinda 109

19. Irrfan Khan 113

20. Johnny Lever 119

21. Mithun Chakraborty 125

22. Manoj Kumar 131

Dedication

"Dedicated to those who failed many a times, but never lost heart and realised the success they dreamt for because they knew that Rome was not built in a day."

Few Words...

You can try and achieve, and believe in. We have several examples in the world. By reading these inspiring stories, see how these people, from the Indian film industry, have achieved their goals. Although their goals were different from each other, and some may seem easy while other hard. But for these people, the goals were 'important' and achieving those was the greatest success for them.

Being focused, and working steadily towards their goals, they overcame all obstacles and hindrances. The never-say-die attitude of these men and women will always serve as an inspiration for generations to come, and make them the 'real heroes'.

This is a iconic capsule collection of the inspirational lives of a few of the many Bollywood stars. The lives have been inspirational and there is no intention to hurt the sentiments of anyone related to it or those who are mentioned in it. It is an ode to the wonderful talent in the world of cinema. Celluloid has the maximum influence on the lives of people, and care has been taken, not to include any material which can or may cause any such problem whatsoever.

Hoping this work finds appreciation in the hearts of cinema lovers... and all.

–Dinesh Verma

Some succeed because they are destined.
Some succeed because they are determined.

Introduction

Life is tough for those born with a failure, traumatic for those whom disability strikes like a bolt from the blue, and a catastrophe for those who cannot cope with such an eventuality. Featured here is a cross section of amazing Indian celebrities from the Indian film fraternity who have managed to achieve the impossible in the face of great disappointment and failure.

These are but a few of the numerous people who have a 'never-say-die' spirit Bollywood stars who have battled disappointment and gone on to shine in their respective careers or taken up an alternative challenge. Hats off to the brave stars featured here and those not featured here who live and lead by example!

Acknowledgements

I am but a medium... the true writer of this work is the almighty, without whose blessings and guidance, the book could have never taken shape. After all, man proposes and HE disposes...

I would like to put in my appreciation and acknowledgement for some people without whom the project wouldn't have seen light. Firstly, I would like to thank Mr. Mukesh Kulothia (Author of the Book "Move Mountains-One Story at a Time") for giving his valuable suggestions. My parents, Mr. Mahesh Chand and Mrs. Bimla Devi, for their constant support and trust in me. My wife, Mrs. Anita Verma and my daughters, Tanya Verma and Bhuvi Verma for standing by me through thick and thin.

This would be incomplete if I don't mention the motivational Mr. Akshar Yadav, Dr. A.K. Saini, Dr. V.K. Goswami, my friends Mr. Ashutosh Kant (Connector & Influencer), Mr. Rakesh Arya (CEO, RDx), Mr. Sanjay Kumar (India's No.1 Lead Expert For Real Estate Tycoons), Mr. Vivek Pathak (Certified Financial Planner), Ms. Rekha Sorout (Women Entrepreneur and Marketing Consultant), Ashish Sapra (Travel Guru, Founder and Owner of Hori Zons Holidays), Mr. Chandan

Goyal (Co-founder of Blue Consulting Pvt. Ltd.) Author of "How to Manufacture Time", Mr. Rohit Nagia Eminent Builder & Author of "Make Your Building for Free", Mr. Rakesh Sharma Indias No.1 Succession Planing Expert and many others who are directly or indirectly related to this endeavour.

No work can find success without the most important part, that is, YOU, The Readers. I wholeheartedly thank the readers for having spent their precious time in giving this work a fair reading. Life is a struggle, and we need to consistently work, and grab the opportunities that come in our way and set parameters for our achievements and goals. The work is especially dedicated to those, who see success not as a destination, but as a journey and a way of life.

–Dinesh Verma

Amitabh Bachchan

I am not different from any other.

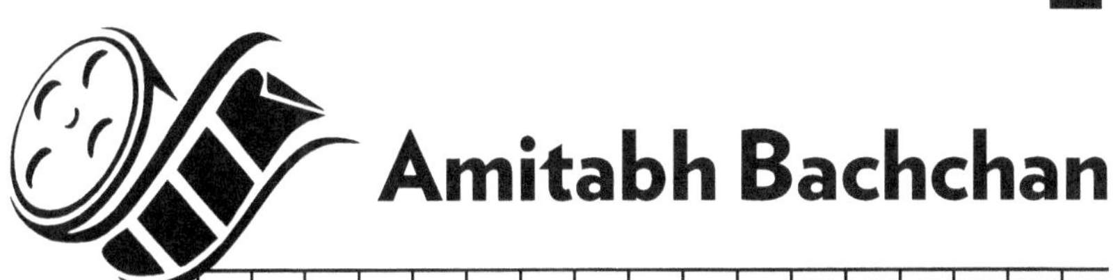

Amitabh Bachchan (born on 11 October, 1942 in Allahabad) has got the distinction of being the Star of the Millennium. Regarded as one of the most respected actors in the world, Amitabh Bachchan is the face of Indian Cinema. He is the Living Legend of the Hindi Film Industry.

*When people see a legend, they call it a legend.
But to be a legend, it's a lot of hard work and
patience. You can't play for five or ten years
and be a legend. It takes longer than that.*

–Burning Spear

He is more impressive than all the Bollywood stars put together. His dynamism and receptive attitude play a major role in his success. It is rare to find an 'actor', in so much demand even at his age. He is one of those, who command respect. He is a legend and an institution in himself.

Amitabh Bachchan is a watershed in the history of Hindi Cinema. It won't be an exaggeration to say that the three major developments in Hindi cinema have been the coming of sound, the advent of colour and the emergence of Amitabh Bachchan. Before he straddled the screen like a colossus, Hindi cinema had never looked as big and significant. Though there had been blockbusters aplenty and big stars but there was no one quite like Amitabh Bachchan. Amitabh Bachchan is a superstar in the truest sense of the word. His name and face have taken over the hearts of minds of people around the world for almost 50 years.

Because you are women, people will force their thinking on you, their boundaries on you. They will tell you how to dress, how to behave, who you can meet and where you can go. Don't live in the shadows of people's judgement. Make your own choices in the light of your own wisdom.

–Amitabh Bachchan

He first gained popularity in the early-1970s as the "angry young man" of Hindi cinema, and has since become one of the most prominent figures, not only in the history of Indian cinema, but globally.

Mr. Bachchan has won numerous awards in his career, including four National Awards, three of which are in the Best Actor category, and fourteen Filmfare Awards. He is the most-nominated performer in any major acting category at Filmfare, with 36 nominations overall. In addition to acting, Bachchan has worked as a playback singer, film producer, and television presenter, and was an elected member of the Indian Parliament from 1984 to 1987.

"No one can go through life without their share of knocks. I am no different from any other"

After taking sabbatical from acting which also witnessed the start of his own company Amitabh Bachchan Corporation Limited ABCL, he was back with a bang. With few ups and downs, he recovered lost ground after the stupendous success of the tele-show *Kaun Banega Crorepati* which he successfully anchored.

SOME MOST INTERESTING FACTS ABOUT AMITABH

1. Amitabh is ambidextrous, he can write with both hands equally well

2. His father wanted to name him Inquilab which means 'revolution' but later named him Amitabh which means 'brilliance unlimited'

3. Amitabh wanted to become an Indian Air Force Officer, but he could not pursue that dream doggedly

4. During his struggling days, Amitabh had spent a few nights on a bench at Marine Drive, Mumbai

5. During the shooting of the movie *'Khuda Gawah'* opposite Sri Devi, the then President of Afghanistan provided Amitabh with half of his country's air force for protection. The movie became one of the most-watched Indian films in the history of Afghanistan

6. For Amitabh Bachchan, the most beautiful actress in the film industry is Waheeda Rahman

7. He is the first Asian actor to have a wax model displayed at Madame Tussaud's in London

> ***I am not conscious of the fact that something special should be done for me.***
>
> ***–Amitabh Bachchan***

8. He was voted 'Star of the Millennium' by BBC online above legends like Laurence Olivier, Charlie Chaplin and Marlon Brando.

9. Amitabh started his career in 1969 as a voice narrator in Mrinal Sen's Bhuvan Shome.

10. Amitabh's actual surname was Srivastav. Later his father adopted his pen name, Bachchan.

11. Amitabh has played the maximum number of double roles in Hindi film industry.

12. Amitabh's first salary was Rs. 300.

13. Amitabh and Rajiv Gandhi were childhood friends. When Sonia Gandhi had visited India in 1968, she was put up at Bachchan's residence.

14. Bachchan is complete vegetarian. He does not even drink tea, coffee or take alcohol. He is also a non-smoker.

15. Amitabh is known to suffer from Asthma. He also has a rare muscular disorder known as myasthenia gravis.

16. Mr. Bachchan is the most followed Bollywood celeb on Twitter, Facebook and even on his blog.

> ***I'd like to believe that tomorrow is another challenge for me. I'm sure there is lot more for me to do, because there is lots and lots of stuff still to be explored.***
>
> ***–Amitabh Bachchan***

Did you know?

The reigning superstar of Bollywood in the 1970s, Big B's magnificent run came to a stop when he met with a near-fatal accident on the sets of the film *Coolie*. Though he miraculously recovered after a long hospitalization, he was not fit enough to carry on acting like in his early days.

He also resumed acting thanks to his great will power, resilience and strong support from family and friends.

Recently, Amitabh was diagnosed with liver cirrhosis, a result of the Coolie accident. Unfortunately, one of the donor's blood was infected with Australian antigen hepatitis. But Big B is braving the malady with a smile and in addition to blogging, he has started tweeting as well. Strong oration, confidence, and knowledge are his key strengths.

On asking, "Do you want to live a life of impact, influence and inspiration like Amitabh Bachchan?" Most of us would respond a resounding "Yes". But are we willing to put in that kind of hard work and live the life of love with work. The only area where Mr. Bachachan is not doing well is following the advice of bed rest from the doctors. He has suffered from asthma and met with many accidents during the shooting of many movies and hence has been on and off medicines and care of doctors. Yet, his passion for work is exemplary. Even at the age of 77 years, with so many surgeries and medical restrictions; this actor can go on for 18 hours straight to work. Once, after returning from hospital he had mentioned "some saints in white coats and stethoscopes have advised me to take more rest but I would continue doing my best and working as much as I can." Amitabh Bachchan is undoubtedly and epitome of inspiration. If you want to learn one thing from Big B, let that be "Finding Joy In Work" and if you have the appetite to learn another – that will without doubt be 'Self Discipline'. Hats off to this God of Indian Cinema!

There is no work without work.

– Amitabh Bachchan

* * *

2

Dilip Kumar

I think personality correction is
necessary for successful people.

The Devdas of Indian cinema, Dilip Kumar was the first star of Indian Cinema. A handsome young man with an X-factor, he has been one of the most influential men of the Indian cinema.

Born on 11 December, 1922 in Peshawar (Now in Pakistan) in a Pashtun family, he was named Muhammad Yusuf Khan. One of the 12 children born to his parents, he adopted his screen name as Dilip Kumar. He worked along with his brother Nasir Khan in films like *Ganga Jamuna* (1961) and *Bairaag* (1976). His father was a fruit merchant and owned orchard in Peshawar and Deolali in Maharashtra.

> *"I have never considered any film*
> *crucial to the progress of my career.*
> *With every film, I discovered my*
> *potential as an actor"*

> **The will to win, the desire to succeed, the urge**
> **to reach your full potential... these are the keys**
> **that will unlock the door to personal excellence.**
>
> **–Confucius**

THE JOURNEY BEGINS

It was destiny that introduced Dileep to Bollywood. He was running a canteen in Pune when director Amiya Chakravarty happened to notice him. It was on the insistence of Chakravarty and Devika Rani, the leading lady of Bollywood in those days that he joined the film industry with the name of Dilip Kumar.

"I think personality correction is necessary for successful men, It's essential one should keep an eye on one's personality"

Dilip Kumar has been widely appreciated for his concern over social causes and has donated a major sum of his earnings for the deprived and the poor. He was awarded the prestigious

Padma Bhushan in 1991, Dada Saheb Phalke Award in 1994 & Padma Vibhushan in 2015 for his valuable contribution to Indian Cinema. Not only in India the actor was worshipped in Pakistan as well. He was recorded the highest civilian honor of Nishan-e-Pakistan by the Government of Pakistan in 1998. He served as the Member of Parliament of India 2000.

He made his debut with Amiya Chakravarty's *Jwar Bhata* in 1944 where he played the protagonist, a wandering musician. His next releases *Pratima* (1945), *Milan* (1947) and *Jugnu* (1947) were also a major hit at the box office.

> *I don't believe you have to be better than*
> *everybody else. I believe you have to be*
> *better than you ever thought you could be.*
>
> *– Dilip Kumar*

He was paired opposite his real-life love Kamini Kaushal in 1948 release *Shaheed* that was based on the freedom movement in India. He worked with Nargis in *Mela* (1948) and only once with Raj Kapoor in *Andaz* in 1949. In 1950s, Dilip Kumar ruled the box-office with his hits like *Arzoo* (1950), *Deedar* (1952), *Aan* (1952) and *Footpath* (1953).

HITTING THE MILESTONE

Dilip Kumar appeared in one of his most remarkable roles in

1955 in Bimal Roy's *Devdas* in which he was paired opposite Suchitra Sen and Vyjayanthimala.

> *"I'm a difficult man and I take-off
> rather slowly. But once I take-off, I
> don't have any difficulty"*

His next release *Naya Daur* that came in 1957 was a huge success both commercially as well as critically.

He delivered his another memorable performance playing Prince Saleem in K Asif's 1960 epic saga *Mughal-e-Azam*. After a series of flops, Dilip Kumar rocked the box-office for one more time with *Ram Aur Shyam* in 1967. He bid adieu to film industry for a while after *Bairaag* in 1976.

He made a comeback with Manoj Kumar's *Kranti* in 1981. The multi-starrer *Kranti* had Manoj Kumar, Hema Malini, Shashi Kapoor, Prem Chopra, Shatrughan Sinha, and Parveen Babi and was one of the biggest hits.

He featured along with Amitabh Bachchan in Ramesh Sippy's Shakti that went on to win the Filmfare Best Movie Award. He got the chance to work again with Nutan in Subhash Ghai's Karma in 1986.

> *"I thought discretion was the better
> part of valor"*

In 1991 in another Subhash Ghai venture *Saudagar*, Dilip Kumar shared screen space with Raaj Kumar. *Qila* that came in 1998, where he played the antagonist, was the last movie of the star.

Dilip Kumar holds the record of winning the most number of Filmfare Best Actor Awards till date. He has won it for *Daag, Azaad, Devdas, Naya Daur, Kohinoor, Leader, Ram Aur Shyam,* and *Shakti.* He was also the first actor to win it in this category and also holds the record of most number of nominations. He was felicitated with the Filmfare Lifetime Achievement Award in 1993.

Do you know?

Dilip Kumar was running an Army Canteen in Pune for the British soldiers before being spotted by director Amaya Chakravarty. He earned a monthly pay of mere Rs. 36 and sold fruits in part time to earn his livelihood.

*A friend is the one who comes in when
the whole world has gone out.*

– Dilip Kumar

Dileep Kumar was initially looking for the job of a writer but after being noticed by Devika Rani he was offered his first role as a male lead in Jawar Bhata in 1944. He initially got a salary of Rs. 1,000 per month and an additional Rs. 200 as a war allowance.

*"Desire is the starting point of all achievement,
not a hope, not a wish, but a keen pulsating
desire which transcends everything".*

* * *

3

Akshay Kumar

*The day I take either my body or my work
for granted will be the day you hear that I've
smashed every inch of myself to pieces.*

–Akshay Kumar

Born as Rajiv Hari Om Bhatia on 9 September, 1967 in Punjab, Amritsar. Akshay Kumar's journey to stardom has been an interesting one and can easily fit as the plot for any Bollywood movie. His father was an Army officer and mother Alka was a home maker. After spending initial years of his childhood in Delhi, Akshay's family moved to Mumbai. He later moved to Bangkok to learn martial arts. He was working as a martial arts instructor in Mumbai when destiny happened to knock his door and he got his first modeling assignment.

> ***The only thing that overcomes***
> ***hard luck is hard work.***
>
> *–Harry Golden*

THE STRUGGLE BEGINS

Akshay made his Bollywood debut with *Saugandh* in 1991. His next release, action thriller *Khiladi*, was an immense hit in the box office. Hereafter he appeared in several movies of the

Khiladi series and all of them performed fair enough in the box-office.

For the next few years, Akshay continued to do action movies till he was approached for Yash Chopra's *'Dil To Pagal Hai'* in 1997. Akshay played the supporting lead in the movie and established himself as a romantic hero. His roles in movies like *Sangharsh* and *Janwar* earned him critical acclaims.

HITTING THE MILESTONE

Akshay tried his hands on comedy with Priya Darshan's *'Hera Pheri'* in 2000 which was a super hit. He was also widely appreciated for his role in Abbas Mastan's directorial *Ajnabee.* He received his first Filmfare Award in the negative role category for the movie.

> *"I am not hungry for success. I am only*
> *hungry for good work, and that is how it is*
> *with most superstars. Every day I tell myself*
> *how fortunate I am to be where I am."*

Akshay has been keen on performing the stunts himself in his films. His daring to perform those dangerous actions himself has earned him the reputation of being the "Jackie Chan of Indian Cinema".

He made his Television debut in 2008 hosting the show, Fear Factor – *Khatron Ke Khiladi.* In 2009 he turned producer establishing his own banner called the Hari Om Entertainment Production Company, named after his late father.

Known by the nicknames like Mr Khiladi, King Kumar and the Best Entertainer, Akshay today lists among one of the highest-paid actors in Bollywood and one of the most influential stars with a huge fan following.

> *I hate partying. If I'm forced to go*
> *to a party or a social gathering, I go*
> *in at 9:30 and leave at 10 P.M.*
>
> *–Akshay Kumar*

The University of Windsor felicitated Kumar with an Honorary Degree of Law in 2008 for his contribution towards the Indian Cinema. In 2009, Government of India recognized his works with the Padma Shri Award.

He is married to Twinkle Khanna, the daughter of Bollywood superstar Rajesh Khanna and Dimple Kapadia. They have a son Aarav born in September, 2002 and a daughter Nitara born in September, 2012.

Do you know?

Rajiv Hari Om Bhatia was working as a Chef in Bangkok before moving to India. He was teaching Martial Arts in Mumbai when one of his students, who also happened to be a photographer, advised him to take up modeling as a career.

Akshay married yesteryear superstar Rajesh Khanna's daughter Twinkle. His wife has always compared his stardom with that of her legendary father.

Interesting Quote

You gain strength, courage and confidence by every experience in which you really stop to look fear in the face. You are able to say to yourself, "I lived through this horror. I can take the next thing that comes along." ...You must do the thing you think you cannot do.

7, 12, 5*40

These are not mere numbers. If you are among those fans of Mr. Khiladi, who want to know as to what time does your favourite hero takes breakfast, at what time he takes lunch, and what is his dinner time, the digits above will suffice.

7: This Box Office Boss takes his breakfast at 7 am.

12: This is the Lunch Time of the Legendary Actor.

5: Do not Surprise, you heard it Right. This is the time he takes his *dinner.

40: He masticates his morsel for 40 times

***He firmly believes that our body does not need
the amount of food that we eat. He advocates
light food in dinner and that too prior to sunset.***

SOME INTERESTING FACTS ABOUT AKSHAY KUMAR

1. Akshay Kumar was a waiter in a restaurant called Metro Guest House, Bangkok.

2. In Bangkok he had posters of Sri Devi, Sylvester Stallone and Jackie Chan, he later worked with all of them.

3. Hosted a Martial Arts documentary titled 'Seven Deadly Arts with Akshay Kumar' for National Geographic Channel.

4. Worked as a light boy for photographer Jayesh Seth in return to shoot his first portfolio.

5. He won the Best Actor award twice—Best Actor in comic and negative role for Garam Masala and Ajnabee respectively.

6. He worked in 8 films with 'Khiladi' in the title---*Khiladi, Main Khiladi Tu Anari, Sabse Bada Khiladi, Khiladiyon*

ka Khiladi, International Khiladi, Mr. and Mrs. Khiladi, Khiladi 420 and *Khiladi 786*.

7. He had a face-off with a shark in South Africa, while shooting for *Ankhen*.

8. He confessed in an interview that he'd steal watches in *Chandani Chowk* just to get some kick in life when he was younger.

9. He nearly broke his back and neck while lifting the 350-pound weighing WWF Champ Underaker in 'Khiladiyon ka Khiladi'.

10. He shot a music video of the Punjabi devotional song, *Nirgun Raakh Liya* and donated all profits to the victims of the train bombings of Mumbai on July 11, 2006.

No one has got close enough to use or abuse me, and even if they did, I wouldn't get too emotional about it. The only thing I ever get emotional about is my family. I am kind to everyone but I trust no one. That keeps me from getting hurt.

* * *

4

Aamir Khan

Aamir Khan was born on 14 March, 1965 in Mumbai. A charismatic actor, an accomplished director and a great philanthropist, Aamir Khan is one of the most accomplished actors in the history of Bollywood. Known for his passion for excellence, he is a synonym of perfection. Aamir Khan has brought a wave of change in the Hindi Cinema and contemporary Indian society with his movies.

*"Film making is like fighting a war
with leadership at the front"*

**A leader is one who knows the way,
goes the way, and shows the way.**

–John C. Maxwell

Aamir Khan was born in a traditional Muslim household. The family traces its roots to the great freedom fighter Maulana Abul Kalam Azad. The star has Bollywood blood running in his veins, with his father Tahir Hussain as one of the acclaimed directors and producers of his time and uncle Nassir Hussain being an accredited producer and actor.

THE STRUGGLE BEGINS

With such a pedigree, Aamir Khan was destined to be a big name in Bollywood. He started his career at a young age of eight. He made his debut as a child artist in 1973 along with his cousin Tariq in Nasir Hussain's directorial *Yadon Ki Baraat*. Aamir Khan made his official entry into the Indian Cinema with Ketan Mehta's Holi in 1984. But it was the 1988 blockbuster *Qayamat Se Qayamt Tak* that established him as an actor in Hindi Cinema. The movie was a huge commercial success and Aamir received his first Filmfare award as Special Jury Award for it. With this, a sparkling new star was born in Bollywood.

"I know I have been very successful in the yesteryears but that's not what it's all about. You can be successful and unfulfilled. As an actor there's still a lot I can learn and do for myself."

Journey to stardom has still not been easy for Amir Khan. His career failed to take off even after his acting skills were widely recognized. Most of his initial films failed miserably at the box office.

Fail Fast, Fail Differently, Fail Forward

–Dinesh Verma

Aamir Khan witnessed success and fame finally with the release of *Dil* in 1990. He was paired against Madhuri Dixit in *Dil* and the movie turned out to be an overnight success. Mahesh Bhatt directorial *Dil Hai Ki Manta Nahi* became the next phenomenal film. It had Amir opposite Mahesh's daughter Puja Bhatt. He was the main lead in 1992 blockbuster *Jo Jeeta Wohi Sikandar* and 1993 romantic family drama *Hum Hain Rahi Pyar Ke.* Both these movies were immense commercial and critical hits.

HITTING THE MILESTONE

Aamir was by now established in Bollywood as the 'chocolate hero.' But the industry saw the emergence of brand Aamir with the release of Ram Gopal Verma's *Rangeela*. Paired opposite Urmila Matondkar, Aamir rocked the Dolby Screen with his incredible performance. Record-breaking melodrama Raja Hundustani hit the floors in 1996. Amir's power-packed performance and sizzling chemistry with Karishma Kapoor was widely acclaimed. The movie bagged him the Filmfare Best Actor Award after being nominated seven times previously. He had finally succeeded in making his presence felt in Bollywood.

> ***I do what I feel is right. I am not scared to
> walk on the new path and take risk.***
>
> ***–Aamir Khan***

However, this period of success was short lived for Aamir. His next few releases could witness only partial success. His work was recognized in the multi-starrer comedy *Ishq* while his impressive performance in *Ghulam* could make the movie only a moderate hit. Even though his films were not doing great at box-office, what couldn't remain unnoticed from the critics and cinema experts was Aamir's Quest for Quality. During an era when every star was busy signing as many assignments as they could, Amir made a difference saying yes only to the movies with a good subject and juicy roles. His commitment to taking up one assignment at a time further proved his professionalism and established him as a 'Serious Actor'. His knack of living the role he did (in *Mangal Pandey, 3 Idiots, Dangal,* etc.) is another virtue associated with Aamir Khan than makes him get an edge over other actors.

He was critically acclaimed for his role of a righteous Police Officer in *Sarfarosh* in 1999 and offbeat film *Earth*. He teamed up with his real brother Faisal Khan for his first release in the new millennium, Mela. But the movie failed to woo audiences.

"I have an enormous amount of stamina."

Aamir Khan created history as the producer and protagonist in Ashutosh Gowarikar's *Lagaan.* He was paired against debutant Gracy Singh in what is accredited as one of the greatest movies of Hindi Cinema. Apart from winning his second Filmfare Award for best performance, the movie was also nominated for Academy Awards for the

best Foreign Language Film. It is the only third Indian movie after *Mother India* (1957) and *Salaam Bombay* (1988) to be nominated for this prestigious award.

His next release, Farhan Akhtar directorial debut *Dil Chahta Hai* was a smashing hit. Co-starring Saif Ali Khan, Akshaye Khanna, Preity Zinta, Dimple Kapadia and Sonali Kulkarni, the movie emerged as a trendsetter. Winning the heart of the youth, it was about love and friendship. His role was widely appreciated for the 2005 period film *Mangal Pandey*. Playing the character of the hero of 1857 Revolt, he experimented with his looks for the first time. This Ketan Mehta biopic had Rani Mukerji and Amisha Patel as the lady leads.

When his career was at its peak, Aamir was undergoing turmoil on the personal front. Aamir and his wife for 15 years,

Reena Dutta developed a rift during the making of *Lagaan*. Reena was his childhood sweetheart and together they had two beautiful children, a son Junaid and a daughter Ira. As he had married Reena going against his family, parting ways with her was definitely not easy for an emotional Aamir. But, he finally ended his marital bond with his wife in the year 2005 with a heavy heart. He married with Kiran Rao, the assistant director of *Lagaan* in the same year(2005). He got involved in the legal battle with his father for the custody of his brother Faisal. But, he lost the case in 2007.

> ***"I enjoyed directing as much as I
> enjoyed acting. For me, work should be
> enjoying and that keeps me going"***

> *The happiness of one's life depends upon
> the quality of his thoughts and work*

Turmoil in Aamir's personal life didn't deter him and he went on to deliver hits after hits. He raised his voice against corruption in 2006 with his release *Rang De Basanti*. This movie touched the heart of every Indian. He won the Filmfare Critics Award for the Best Actor. This was followed by *Fanaa* in which he was paired against Kajol. Aamir played the lead role in his directorial venture *Tare Zamin Par*. He made parents across the nation think about parenting ways through this movie. For the strong message it conveyed, it got exemption from taxes in many states. It earned him the Filmfare Best Director and the Best Movie Award.

He appeared in *Ghajini* in 2008 that turned out to be the greatest hit of the year.

His role as Ranchodas Chanchad in *3 Idiots* was a head-turning one. The movie became one of the biggest commercial hits and set up new benchmarks for Indian cinema. His movie *Talaash* was a box-office hit in 2012 while *Dhoom 3* at the end of 2013 was a massive commercial hit. In the next year, he played a titular alien in the movie *PK*. This film did US $ 110 Million business and Aamir got the nomination for the Filmfare Award for the Best Actor. In the year 2016, Khan played the father of two young female wrestlers in the sports biopic *Dangal*. This film got the Filmfare award for the best film and Aamir Khan received the Filmfare Award for the best actor.

Aamir Khan made his television debut in 2012 with the show *Satyamev Jayate*. This show focused on sensitive social issues prevalent in India, such as criminalization of politics, female foeticide, honour killing, child sexual abuse, domestic violence, rape, etc.

Do you know?

Aamir Khan has taken his inspiration from Alfred Hitchcock's movies.

This great actor from Bollywood has earned many many accolades for his humility. He has kept away from the glamorous award ceremonies and has refused all of them. He even said no for a wax replica of him being placed at the prestigious Madame Tussauds London.

This perfectionist Khan has insisted on completed scripts being presented to him before committing to any film and takes up one project at a time. These trends are quite unusual in the business of Bollywood where every actor is thronged with multiple assignments at a time and scripts details being often improvised on the day of shooting.

> ***Perfection is achieved, not when there***
> ***is nothing more to add, but when***
> ***there is nothing left to take away.***

Before I close the brief story of Aamir Khan. Let me present top 6 lesson to you from this super-star's all-time blockbusters:

1. **Ghajini:** 'विश्वास और घमंड में बहुत कम फर्क है, मैं कर सकता हूँ, यह विश्वास है, सिर्फ मैं ही कर सकता हूँ, यह घमंड है।'

2. **Rang De Basanti:** 'जिंदगी जीने के दो ही तरीके होते हैं–(1) जो हो रहा है होने दो, बर्दाश्त करते जाओ या फिर (2) जिम्मेदारी उठाओ उसे बदलने की'।

3. **3 Idiots:** 'बच्चा, काबिल बनो, काबिल, कामयाबी तो साली झक मार के पीछे भागेगी'।

4. **Ghulam:** 'लडेंगे तो खून बहेगा... नहीं लडेंगे तोह ये लोग खून चूस लेंगे।

5. **Taare Zamin par:** अपनी महत्वाकांक्षाओं का वजन अपने बच्चों के नाजुक कंधों पे डालना ... ये बाल मजदूरी से भी बुरा है।

6. **Dangal:** 'मैं हमेशा ये सोच के रोता रहा कि लड़का होता तो देश के लिए कुश्ती में गोल्ड लाता, ये बात मेरे समझ में नहीं आयी, कि गोल्ड तो गोल्ड होता है, लड़का लाए या लड़की'।

* * *

5

Salman Khan

I know my potential and my limitations.

"Turn your nightmares into your dreams, some dreams don't turn out the way you want them to, then wake up and turn them around in your favor"

To accomplish great things, we must dream as well as act.

–Anatole France

Born on 27 December, 1965, Salman Khan is the son of the legendary writer Salim Khan, who penned many super hits in the yesteryears. Salman started his acting career in 1988 with a supporting role in the movie *Biwi Ho To Aisi*. The following year he had the leading role in the Box Office romantic hit *Maine Pyar Kiya*. A movie that created history. From there, he became the heartthrob of Indian cinema lovers.

Often known as Bollywood's 'bad boy', his knack of walking into trouble has overshadowed people's perception of him as an actor. He has been featured as the bad guy of the industry several times over. But many-a-common-man claims that this macho hunk has a heart made of pure gold.

> *I no longer do a film for the wrong reasons. I have to be convinced ethically and morally. Both the director and I have to be on the same page. There are just five songs in most films these days, and they have to be amazing. There has to be a twist in the screenplay. The editing has to be crisp. Your hard work should show, but effortlessly.*
>
> *–Salman Khan*

Following this with other Box Office hits he showed his terrific performance in *Saajan* (1991), *Andaz Apna Apna* (1994), *Hum Aapke Hain Koun* (1994), *Karan Arjun* (1995), *Khamoshi*: The Musical (1996), *Kuch Kuch Hota Hai* (1998) and many more movies. His transformations can be a sensitive, vulnerable, funny to an aggressive and charming man as per the demands of the role.

In 2003, he gave his emotionally charged performance by playing an obsessed lover in *Tere Naam* (2003) that translated into good reviews and a good run at the box office. He not only managed to revive his career, but also was able to restore the confidence of his producers and distributors alike.

> ***"For me acting comes straight from the heart. In that sense I don't act at all. I think that to feel the character's pain I have to be myself. Somewhere audiences see that"***

His work was noticed internationally in the movie *Phir Milenge* (2004) where he played the role of an AIDS patient. It was well appreciated by the World Health Organization (WHO) for presenting the problems of AIDS patients in today's world. He agreed to work for 'Revathi' without even charging anything for the movie, as it was on a social cause.

He happily accepted the role, which had been turned down by many Bollywood actors.

In 2007, he launched 'Being Human – Salman Khan Foundation'. This charitable organisation aids the underprivileged in areas such as education and health care.

> *"My strength lies in the fact that I know*
> *my potential and my limitations, I*
> *don't do what I can't. I turn down parts*
> *that I know will suit others better"*

More recently, he starred in the multiple record-breaking Box Office super-hit *Dabangg* (2010). His performance and dance style are full of ease, and are unique.

> ***A lion runs the fastest when he is***
> ***hungry. Know your power and run to***
> ***achieve your objectives of life.***
>
> ***–Salman Khan***

Salman Khan has simply proved to the world that he is not to be taken lightly. Amongst all the heavy-weight Khans, he is the coolest Khan around. ***"Salman is a philanthropist, and he has a heart of Gold."***

DID YOU KNOW?

There were a lot of inside stories coming out about how Salman Khan is a very kind at heart and how he always looks after everyone like a big brother and takes care of them.

This once angry young man has truly proved to the world that he has a soft mushy heart deep inside which is being adored by one and all in the film industry.

Thus, whenever the new generation of actors is asked about Salman Khan, every time they come up with some real-life experiences of how Salman Khan made sure that there was proper pampering on the sets, etc.

He is respected truly for the positive attitude that he has. He has never been caught with any negative statements about any of his colleagues or co-stars. He is as chilled as a teenager. He does not believe in creating ill will, as it is well known that he forgives and forgets things and is always ready to hug and make up.

Salman Khan's kind streak is also evident in his social work. Every day there are stories about how he gave cycles to some children on the streets, how he gave a bundle of notes to someone who had been struggling for years and many things like that. His setting up of the 'Being Human' foundation is also a great way for him to give whatever he can to help the poor and the downtrodden.

He is conscientious to acknowledge and give credit to the deserving. He recently introduced and endorsed the uniform of his bodyguard, who has been with him for a good many years, for his movie - 'Bodyguard'. It is a noble gesture indeed.

> *To do something, however small, to make others happier and better, is the highest ambition, the most elevating hope, which can inspire a human being...!*

Salman Khan is undoubtedly the most popular actor in Bollywood. Despite commanding a huge fan following across the nation, he is known to be very humble and down-to-earth. Being a celebrity, he was never free from controversies. However, the actor has taken all of that in his stride and come out as a better human being every time. Not only facing the fears and failures head on but also coming out as a stronger and better person from each of the struggles is something worth learning from him. Though he has made his share of mistakes in life yet he wants to be remembered not for his acting but for his deeds which make the world a better place.

He was born to a Hindu mother and a Muslim father with an added love from his second mother who is a Christian. In fact during his school days, once he was asked by a teacher that what religion does he belong to? To which Salman responded 'Human, I am a human first.' Not being bound by any religion instead imbibing the best from each of the religions is yet another thing worth learning from him. Salman Khan's Ganesh Puja celebration is not only worth talking but a lot more. Let there be harmony inside the hearts and outside in the world.

Oh yes, nothing great was ever achieved without massive action. Salman is a firm believer in working so hard and achieving success which is worth praising by friends and foes.

Salman was quoted as saying, "Have you seen a duck gliding smoothly in water? Does it ever look like it is paddling furiously underneath the surface? I don't have to show that I am working very hard."

In nutshell, it won't be wrong if I make an equation:

World Class Attitude + Hard Work = Salman Khan

* * *

6

Shah Rukh Khan

The dream I chased, took me on a journey. A journey more rewarding than the goals.

Shahrukh Khan was born on 2 November 1965 in New Delhi. A guy who is so obsessed with his girlfriend that he came to Mumbai and searched for his love with only the information that she loved swimming. He is none other than Shah Rukh Khan.

"Walk on with hope in your heart, and you'll never walk alone"

He sold his Pentax camera for Rs. 10,000, as he combed beaches with hope and prayer that he would locate her, somewhere sleeping on the park benches, and cleaning and bathing in the hotel bathrooms. His friends lost hope and purchased tickets with the petty amount left, while he, for the last time combed the north Mumbai beaches and luckily found her.

From being boy next door, to be labeled as 'King Khan', the journey has not been a simple one. In his first castings for a movie produced and directed by Arundhati Roy, he was given a role of an extra and he vowed that he would one day win an Oscar. Such was the confidence and determination in him.

He was recommended for the role of Abhimanyu Rai (*Fauji*) by the son-in-law of the producer who was showing some flats to his mother. The original choice of the main lead was the producer's son who was also the camera man in the serial.

However, Shah Rukh got the role as there was a logistic problem of handling the camera and the role was simultaneously left by the producer's son. Little did the world know, that it was the making of a superstar...

His role became bigger gradually as the other co-stars threw tantrums while he worked hard to get the nuances right as an army officer. And as they say, rest is history.

Not being the first choice but always the second or the third choice continued with the movie *Baazigar* also, where the other established stars like Aamir, Anil Kapoor were the first choice, but they refused to do the movie where the protagonist had negative traits and kills without any compunctions and "is a murderer in the movie", and had negative connotations, as a villain.

The same continued with *Darr* where he was selected with great reluctance, as no established actor of that era wanted to be seen being beaten to pulp at the end in the movie. It was an obvious clash between the heroic images that the Indian Cinema boasted of. Juhi Chawla, the reigning superstar shrieked as she was persuaded by the director/producer that this actor was going to be another Aamir Khan in making, when she met him for the first time during the shooting of *Darr*. They became close family friends over the years. Both the movies were blockbusters and he went on to bag the Filmfare award for Best Actor for *Baazigar*. He went to meet Abbas-Mastan (directors of *Baazigar*) after the ceremony at their residence and touched their feet. Such was his humility. The attitude of a person with no power in hands, and the attitude which 'film' covers to him, is the true reflection of his attitude.

> *"You never win the silver. You only lose*
> *the gold."*

Shah Rukh Khan initially refused to do *Dilwale Dulhania Le Jayenge* with Aditya Chopra as he thought of it as a romantic cliché. He only agreed to do it as he liked the last scene where the father lets go of the heroine's hand undoubtedly a very popular scene of the movie.

Initially, he never wanted to be a Bollywood star but a television personality like Oprah Winfrey and refused movies in the beginning. His fiancé and later his wife, Gauri, had strong reservations against him joining Bollywood. It must have been hard to make the king of his heart, into the 'King of Bollywood'.

On the personal front, he also refused to tell a lie to his in-laws who were against his marriage to their Hindu daughter. His fiancé and later wife insisted Shahrukh to tell his in-laws that he had Rs. 6 lacs in his bank when he only had Rs. 28,000 in his bank account. He refused to do so and grandly proclaimed that time, that as Dilip Kumar had become old, Amitabh Bachchan had retired, it was his time now "to be crowned as the king" when he left Delhi for Mumbai to start a career in Bollywood.

"The dream I chased, took me on a journey. A journey more rewarding than the goals, the achievements. When I look back it's like facing a million mirrors. Each reflection opens a window. A window to the world I've just discovered. The world I want to share with all of you."

One of his popular flicks or films, *Chamatkar* was refused by him, as when the producer insisted that he should hide his marriage, as that was the norm at that time. He stood by his stance, and changed the norms. He has been a trendsetter in this regard. He is more than happy in being labeled as a family man, and someone who keeps 'family' at the highest pedestal of his life. He is honest and at times very straightforward also.

He claims that he can do anything for money except films. Films he does only for love. Everyone lines for a passion, and his passion is – Movies.

He also went into production and promised to make different kinds of movies. His first movie *Phir Bhi Dil Hai Hindustani* made with blood and tears, flopped and the critics, media were savage in their attacks. However, it did not deter him, and he further produced movies such as Om Shanti Om which have been super hits. He is rightly known as King Khan.

Do you Know?

Sitting forlornly at the Marine Drive in Mumbai, he promised that one day he would rule the city of Mumbai.

He came to Mumbai to act in a serial and got stranded at the Mumbai airport in the middle of the night as the person who was supposed to pick him overslept, he cried in the telephone booth thinking that probably it was a hoax while searching for some coins.

Juhi Chawla could not get over the fact that he was so dark with wild unruly hair in comparison to Aamir Khan and Salman Khan who were recently launched at the same time.

He grandly declared that if he had to choose between his flourishing career in the movie or his wife, he would always choose his wife over everything else.

Gradually, he became a superstar giving one hit after another. He has always charged lesser than his fellow actors while doing the films as he feels that all the name and fame he has is due to the film industry and makes up with the brand endorsements. He is proud of his hard work and has made others also proud.

> **Cinema in India is like brushing your teeth in the morning. You can't escape it.**
>
> **–Shah Rukh Khan**

> *Most of the important things in the world have been accomplished by people who have kept on trying when there seemed to be no hope at all !*

Shah Rukh Khan is more than just any actor. He is an icon. He is a role model. He is a charmer. With dimples that melt your heart, eyes that make you want to look into them for the rest of your life, voice that touches you deep inside, this man is surely no ordinary entertainer.

He is a living proof of the quote by Bill Gates that 'If you are born poor it's not your fault but if you die poor it's your fault. This man who lost his parents at a very young age and lived for many days by borrowing Rs. 20 every day from his friends has everything a rich person must have.

Dil Wale Dulhaniya Le Jaayenge to *Dil Toh Pagal Hai to Veer Zara to Kuchh Kuchh Hota Hai to Kabhi Khushi Kabhi Gam to Chak De India*. From RaJ Malhotra in *DDLJ* to Hocky Coach Kabir in *Chak De India*, there are so many things we can learn from all his movies and his real life story. Yet, one thing which tops the list is the ability to reinvent yourself every time you meet with failure or unprecedented success. Saying 'Change is the only constant' is cliché but how many of us are committed to change willingly and not get forced or dragged by the change.

Let's embrace change and reinvent ourselves on regular basis. If we can commit to consistently reinventing ourselves we can surprise ourselves on our ability to do things which once seemed impossible.

7

Raj Kapoor

I've struggled a lot for what I have.

The blue-eyed star was born to Prithviraj Kapoor and Ramsarni Devi Kapoor in Dhakki Munawwar Shah in Peshawar in erstwhile British India on 14 December, 1924. He was the eldest of the four children born to his parents. His family came to Bombay in 1929. His brothers Shammi and Shashi Kapoor are both renowned actors.

Raj Kapoor, the showman of Indian cinema was a multi-faceted genius. He has acted, produced and directed some of the greatest Hindi movies of all time.

***The secret of genius is to carry the spirit
of the child into old age, which means
never losing your enthusiasm.***

–Aldous Huxley

THE JOURNEY BEGINS

Raj Kapoor did all odd jobs during the initial days of his career, he was a clap boy assisting director Kidar Sharma. He made his first appearance on the silver screen in 1935 at the age of 11, in the movie Inquilab. He fell in love with actor Prem Nath's sister Krishna Malhotra who happened to be his father's second cousin and his aunt and eventually married her in 1946.

HITTING THE MILESTONE

The following year Raj Kapoor made his debut as the lead in Kidar Sharma's *Neel Kamal*. At the age of 24, in 1948, Raj Kapoor established his studio R.K. Films and became the youngest director of his time. The first film that he made as a director was *Aag* that turned out to be an overnight success.

*"Those days acting was not considered
a respectable profession. Only
prostitutes and other such lower classes
were associated with it"*

From here on, he went on to act and direct in his movies simultaneously. Some of the greatest movies directed by Raj Kapoor were *Barsaat (1949), Awaara (1951), Shri 420 (1955)* and *Sangam (1964)*. He pairing opposite the damsel beauty Nargis became extremely popular. The duo went on to hit the box-office with their portrayal of common man and his issues. The movies appealed to every section of the society during those days.

> **Light comes from the moon and not**
> **the stars ... you can be friends with**
> **one and not with thousands.**
>
> **–Raj Kapoor**

Raj Kapoor had a very profound knowledge of music. His movies were popular for their beautiful memories, not only in India, but also in Soviet Union. He was one among the initial few stars of the Hindi cinema who were recognized internationally. He has been categorized as the 'Charlie Chaplin of India' by the popular film critics and historians. His tramp-like figure and the ability of being honest and jovial at times of great adversity drew such comparisons.

Mera Naam Joker (1970) was his dream project. After its failure in 1970, Kapoor took up subjects moving around romance and sensuality. He introduced his son Rishi Kapoor and Dimple Kapadia in 1973 with the film Bobby. The movie evolved as a trendsetter for teenage romance in Hindi cinema. The film had Dimple in skimpy outfits, which was definitely a bold attempt considering the society in those days. He

raised the art of sensuality further in his movies with his next projects *Satyam Shivam Sundaram (1978)* and *Ram Teri Ganga Maili (1985)*. His movies were with a social message like in *Premrog (1982)* where he advocated widow remarriage.

He was honored with the prestigious Dadasaheb Phalke Award in 1987. He died at the age of 63 in 1988 because of complications arising from asthma. He was working for his film Henna at the time of his death which was later completed by his son Randhir Kapoor. The movie based on the romance of a Pakistani girl and an Indian boy witnessed immense success at the box-office.

He was passionate about cinema and loved every aspect of it. He will get involved even in the minute nitty-gritty of the films that he made. He was a man with a big heart, a true performer and a theatrical genius. However, he knew the harsh reality that no one is indispensable in the world of showbiz, and rightly said in his lines...

"Kal khel mein hum ho na ho,
gardish mein tare rahenge sada..."

He proudly proclaimed, THE SHOW MUST GO ON...

Do you know?

Raj Kapoor was popular not only in India but also in Middle East, the erstwhile Soviet Union, China, the South-East Asia and in large parts of Africa. His movies were an international success.

Raj Kapoor has left behind a rich legacy and a family that is filled with lot of talent. His father, two brothers, both the brothers-in-law, three sons, daughter in laws, sisters-in-law, grandchildren and nephew and nieces and other members of his extended family have been an active part of the Indian film industry.

His grandson Nikhil Nanda, son of his eldest daughter Ritu Kapoor Nanda is married to Shweta, none other than the daughter of legendary Amitabh Bachchan.

"Striving for success without hard work is like trying to harvest where you haven't planted"

Raj Kapoor will always remain the original and greatest showman of Indian cinema. In a span of almost 50 years, he had an illustrious career both in front and behind the camera. He won three National Awards, 11 Filmfare trophies, Padma Bhushan and Dadasaheb Phalke Honours. The Filmfare Lifetime Achievement Award is named after Raj Kapoor.

Do you wonder how could he achieve so much in just one lifetime? I think there were two reasons:

1. He started early. He found his love of life in cinema and appeared as actor for the first time in 1945 in the

film Inquilab in a tender age of just 10 years. Great achievements take time. If you want to accomplish BIG things, start early and persist. Decide to be a master of one field and not jack of all trades. Mastery pays huge dividends over lifetime.

2. Decide fast. If you want to do things .. just get up and do those. Don't linger on decisions and waste time. Raj Kapoor was a fast decision maker. Though he might have made some wrong decisions due to haste but that is how one gains experience. And yes, as you keep on gaining experience the probability of making right decisions keeps on increasing. Just to share one of the incidents where Raj Kapoor decided quickly:

When Raj Kapoor was in the process of finalising the lead actress in his film *'Satyam Shivam Sundaram'* (1978), Zeenat Aman landed up at his office dressed up as a village girl. Not just that she even had the 'burnt face' makeup. He was so impressed with her dedication that he finalised her name for the lead role immediately.

Start Early. Be a Quick Decision Maker.

* * *

8

Mohammed Rafi

*Kisi ka dil hamne kabhi dukhaya
nahin.*

Muhammad Rafi, born on 24 December, 1924 was a singer who is revered by many as one of the greatest singers of the Indian Film industry. He was born in Skotla Sultan Singh in the Punjab province of undivided India. Rafi learnt music from Ustad Bade Ghulam Ali Khan, Ustad Abdul Wahid Khan, Pandit

Jiwan Lal Mattoo and Firoze Nizam. He gave his first stage performance at the tender age of 11.

> ***Music is a higher revelation than all wisdom and philosophy..Music can change the world.***
>
> ***–Ludwig Van Beethoven***

Rafi ruled the heart of millions with the magic of his golden voice. He was called 'The Voice' in popular music circle for his determination to put his heart and soul to the every composition he sang. Rafi's voice was a gift to Indian cinema and his place in the heart of music lovers will continue to be intact for ages to come.

THE STRUGGLE BEGINS

Rafi didn't come from a family of musicians however with his incredible vocal quality he has proven the fact that a star was rising since his infancy. His elder brother Muhammad Deen ran a barber shop. Young Rafi would often found giving company to his brother in his shop. When he was around seven-year-old, there came a faqir who was singing and playing his ektara while walking on the streets. His brother found Rafi following the faqir and soon it became a daily mundane. Rafi would spent hours under huge tree that was the abode of that faqir. One day while Rafi was busy humming one of the tunes he learnt from the faqir, customers at his brother's shop were astonished seeing the talent in the young child. He was singing in the perfect pitch and there was an incredible melody in his voice.

"No one can be a Rafi"   –Naushad

At the age of fifteen Rafi decided to take up singing as a career but his father, the village landlord was mad dead against it. But his elder brother Deen had recognized Rafi's talent and had decided to support him in his endeavor.

Rafi didn't enjoy anything as much he did singing. He gave his voice to a song composed by Shyam Sunder in 1941 for the Punjabi film Gul Baloch at the mere age of seventeen. Overwhelmed by the success of the song, Rafi took the daring step of finding a career for himself in the Hindi Film industry. In 1942 when he arrived in Mumbai, Shaym Sunder again offered him a chance for the Hindi film Gaon Ki Gauri.

After the success of his debut song, Rafi approached Naushad, the renowned music director of his time. He confided in him his admiration to for the Kundan Lal Saigal the great and shared his dream to sing with the legend once. Naushad obliged his request by offering his two lines to sing with K.L. Saigal for Sahjehan. Rafi got the real recognition for his own songs in Baiju Bawra. Naushad made brilliant use of Rafi's vocal quality in this musical movie wherein he sang like *"O duniya ke rakhwale..."* together with *"Man tarpat hari darshan..."* setting up a benchmark of his own.

*"I am pained to see before my eyes,
some singers who, after giving one hit
song, start acting big only to fall down
with a thud soon after"*

HITTING THE MILESTONE

In his career that spans beyond for decades, Rafi sang over 26,000 songs in almost all of the languages in India. He became the voice of every male lead like Shammi Kapoor, Dilip Kumar, Rajendra Kumar, Dev Anand, Dharmendra, Shashi Kapoor, and Raj Kumar during the 1960s. The credit behind the popularity of Shammi Kapoor has been given to Rafi for quite a considerable extent. It is still believed that these were the songs that were sung by Rafi in his distinct manner that took those movies to the zenith of success. His versatility made Shammi the '*Yahoo*' star, Rajendra Kumar the 'Jubilee star' and Jitendra the 'Jumping Jack'. He gave his immortal voice to movies like Basant Bahar, Professor, *Junglee, Suraj, Brahmachari, An Evening in Paris, Dil Tera Deewana, Yakeen, Prince, Love in Tokyo, Beti Bete, Dil Ek Mandir, Dil Apna Aur Preet Parai, Gaban* and *Jab Pyar Kisi Se Hota Hai.*

Rafi's talent was acknowledged by the Government of India when he was conferred with the Padma Shree in 1965. In 1977 he was felicitated with the 'Rajat Kamal Award' at the 25th National Film Festival Awards. A man with tremendous grace and integrity he remained humble and soft spoken even after witnessing such great success.

"किसी का दिल हमने कभी दुखाया नहीं। जो किसी का दिल दुखाता है, वो कभी तरक्की नहीं करेगा जिंदगी में"।

DO YOU KNOW?

Rafi went against his father's wishes to take up singing as his career. An illiterate man, he will keep the words in his memory before approaching the microphone.

He sang songs without taking a fee for the struggling composers.

"Even at the worst there is a way out, a hidden secret that can turn failure into success and despair into happiness. No situation is so dark that there is not a ray of light".

It is acknowledged that he has sung around 26000 songs, but the researchers have found only 7,405 songs. Yet the glory of singing in maximum number of languages by an Indian play back singer goes to Mohammed Rafi with his charming voice, he has sung in 14 Indian languages and 4 foreign languages.

The man who never went to a school for any formal education, how could he do this awesome feat?

Here lies the secret, 'In a fine morning of 1960, the producer of the movie Kohinoor came to visit Rafi with a gift and some flowers .The producer was guilty that initially he refused to incorporate Rafi's song in the movie but in reality the song has worked as the key factor for success of the movie. In response, Rafi accepted only the flowers and rejected the gift. He said that the public has already gifted him by accepting the song and that is the best gift he could get.

What a height of humbleness. Do you know about people who become arrogant and full of ego on some initial success. Authors just don't get tired of speaking about their own books just by publishing books, you tubers just go on and on speaking about virtues of themselves and their content that they don't really have time to think on how create more value for their viewers. Are you also one of such people? If not, bravo! You are on the road to bigger success ahead.

Don't get so busy in talking about your past successes that you have no time to dream and craft your future successes. Rafi Sahab had this habit of being busy with his dreams and left the job of doing the talk to the world.

* * *

9

Asha Bhosle

Asha Bhosle was born in the family of musical legends, on September, 1933 in Sangli, Maharashtra. She is the daughter of Pandit Deenanath Mangeshkar and the younger sister of the Indian nightingale, Lata Mangeshkar.

Asha Bhosle is a playback singer and vocalist. She has been a playback singer in films for nearly six decades, an accomplishment that marked her entry into the Guinness Book of World Records for recording the highest number of songs in music history. There could hardly be an Indian untouched by the magic called Asha Bhosle.

> ***Music is a moral law. It gives soul to the universe,
> wings to the mind, flight to the imagination,
> and charm and gaiety to life and to everything.***
>
> *–Plato*

Though coming from such a powerful family, the path to stardom was still not easy for Asha. Initially compared with her legendary sister and rejected for her shrill voice, Asha lived up to the true meaning of her name which means hope. She kept the struggle going and continued working hard.

> *"I constantly need something new
> and challenging"*

THE JOURNEY BEGINS

Asha lost her father at the age of nine. The family shifted from Pune to Kolhapur and then finally to Mumbai in search of livelihood. Asha fell in love with her sister Lata's secretary Ganpat Rao Bhosle at a very tender age. At sixteen she eloped with the man of her dreams who was fifteen years senior to her to have a family. She had only two sarees as her prized possession and married Bhosle, going against her mother and elder sister's wishes. Life took a bitter turn after marriage. Bhosle not only tortured Asha but it also became difficult for her to make both the ends meet with her three children. The tough times have taken it all from Asha but what remained with her was immense talent as a singer and her indomitable attitude towards life.

> *"I believe in destiny and the philosophy*
> *of karma. Many people have*
> *contributed, but I struggled alone"*

She began her career at the time when it was dominated by legends like her sister Lata Mangeshkar, Geeta Dutt and Shamshad Begum. Songs that came to her kitty were the ones rejected by these singers. She sang only for second lead, vamps and primarily cabaret numbers. She really had to go through an extremely difficult time before she made it to the top.

HITTING THE MILESTONE

Asha got the first major break of her career in the film CID in 1956. Music director O.P. Nayaar saw the talent in her and gave her chance to sing in many of his upcoming films. *Naya Daur* that came in 1957 gave her the long-awaited success. Her pairing with Nayyar resulted in songs like *Aaiye*

*meherban.., Deewana hua badal..., Isharon-isharon mein...,
Aao huzur tumko..., Ude jab-jab zulfein teri....* The last song of
this duo before they parted ways was *Chain se...* from the film
Pran Jaaye Par Vachan Na Jaaye (1974).

> ### With singing, you get lost in the music - I
> ### go into another world when I'm singing.
>
> ### –Asha Bhosle

Sachin Dev Burman along with Asha created soundtracks
for movies that witnessed phenomenal success. Under the
patronage of S.D. Burman, she went on to record some of her
most unforgettable melodies along with Muhammad Rafi and
Kishore Kumar.

After S.D. Burman, she collaborated with his son R.D.
Burman and reached the zenith of her career. She received
widespread accolades for her movie *Teesri Manzil* that came
in 1966. R.D. and Asha paired along in real life as well when
the duo tied the knot in 1980.

Asha gave her voice to Helen, the cabaret queen of Hindi
cinema. Helen was so impressed with Asha's singing style that she
would attend her recordings in studios to understand the mood
of her singing and will choreograph her dance steps accordingly.
Some of the timeless classics that Asha sang for Helen include
*Piya tu ab to aaja... (Caravan), O haseena zulfon wali (Teesri
Manzil),* and Yeh mera dil... (Don). Asha's versatile singing and
immense talent can be seen in songs like *AA Jane Jaan...* from
the movie *Jawaani Diwaani (1972).* The son demanded switch

of pitch from high to low almost simultaneously and Asha has justified it with her incredible talent.

Songs like Dum Maro Dum from the movie Hare Rama Hare Krishna brought before audiences a completely unexplored side of Asha's talent. Her romantic numbers like *Chura Liya Tumne Jo Dil Ko...* from *Yadon Ki Baraat* made her the reputation of being the only playback singer of bollywood with the ability to sing almost all types of songs, including the romantic songs. For her melody *Mera Kuch Saman...* from *Ijaazat* won her second Filmfare best singer award. Her melodious songs continue to move music lovers till today.

She proved her versatility yet another time when she went on to sing Ghazals for the movie *Umrao Jaan*. Khyaam had lowered Asha's pitch for the songs of this movie and what was created is still preserved in history as one of the most remarkable compositions of Hindi Cinema. Her songs of Umrao Jaan that included *"Dil Cheez Kya Hai"*, *"In Aankhon Ki Masti Ke"*, *"Yeh Kya Jagah Hai Doston"* and *"Justaju Jiski Thi"* bagged her first Filmfare Award.

She experimented with her voice yet again singing peppy numbers like *Tanha Tanha, Kambaqt Ishq* and *Chori pe chori*. She also has many pop numbers to her credit and has sung with international sensations like Boy George, Black Eyed Peas, and cricketer Brett Lee, Cold Play, etc.

*"The self-confidence and very strong
will power have stood me in good stead"*

Asha has been felicitated with the Filmfare Awards for eight times, twice with the national awards and with infinite other accolades. Time has been unable to touch the impactful tone of Asha and the octogenarian continues to woo the world with her soulful melodies

Do you know?

Asha along with her sister Lata took up acting and singing as a career to support their family.

A heavily pregnant Asha used to travel by trains to complete her singing assignments and there have been times when upon reaching the venue with so much hardship it was communicated to her that the offer has been given to the singing sensations of the time.

She underwent physical harassment and mental torture in her married life and left home when she was pregnant with her third child Anand.

In the early 1950s, Ash used to get only those projects that have been rejected by singers like Lata Mangeshkar, Geeta Dutt and Shamshad Begum.

> *"Your chances of success in any*
> *undertaking can always be measured by*
> *your belief in yourself".*

She is the legend who has sung over 11,000 songs in more than 20 Indian languages, been immortalized on a UK No 1 record, and found a place in the Guinness Book of World Records as the world's most prolific recording artist.

Asha was also the first Indian singer to be nominated for the prestigious Grammy Award.

A girl whose father died in early childhood. Didn't go to some famous college for education, got married to a man of double her age in just 16 years of age with whom she did not have good time and finally got divorced. How did she manage to be the queen of the singing world?

The answer lies in a single word: COLLABORATIONS

Lets understand every success (even in the fields which require solo performances like sports or singing or acting) depends on the kind of teams we have with us. When you pay to the people who work in your teams they are called your employees and when you earn as well as grow together it's called collaboration.

Asha Bhosle has collaborated with Boy George, Michael Stipe, the Kronos Quartet, Nelly Furtado and Code Red. This list of amazing collaborations started in the 1980s when Asha came together with Stephen Luscombe (of Blancmange) and Vince Clark to form a group called the West India Company. The record released by this group was an unexpected success and was soon followed by other amazing collaborations such as The Way You Dream (a duet with Michael Stipe).

In 1997, British band Cornershop paid a tribute to Asha with their hit number, 'Brimful of Asha'. Interestingly, the Black-Eyed Peas' hit song from 2005, *"Don't Phunk With My Heart,"* was based on samples from two different songs by Asha!

Asha found outlet of her creativity (and unimaginable success) through unique collaborations.

* * *

10

Rajesh Khanna

"It's time for Pack Up".

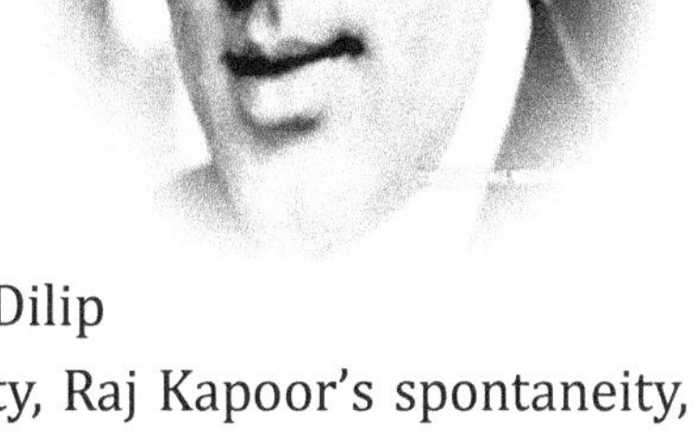

Rajesh Khanna was born as Jatin Khanna on 29 December, 1942 in Amritsar, Punjab and was adopted by his foster parents Chunni Lal Khanna and Leela Wati Khanna. Coming from a simple family, his biological father was headmaster in a local school.

"My inspirations include Dilip Kumar's dedication and intensity, Raj Kapoor's spontaneity, Dev Anand's style and Shammi Kapoor's rhythm"

We're always in the middle of two energies. Gravity is sinking you down; inspiration is pulling you up.

–Mandy Ingber

THE JOURNEY BEGINS

Rajesh Khanna started taking interest in acting since his school days. He played a wounded dumb soldier in a play called "*Andha Yug*", the chief guest advised him to take up acting impressed with his performance.

"I was discovered as an actor at the age of 23 when I won the talent contest. *Aakhri Khat* made me a star. *Aradhana* made me the superstar. Anand made me a legend. *Amar Prem* made me immortal. *Amardeep* ended my bad run at the box office".

He was one of the eight finalists in 1965 of All India Talent Contest organized by United Producers and Filmfare and eventually went on to win it. As a reward he got to appear in Chetan Anand's *Aakhri Khat* (1966) and Ravindra Dave's *Raaz*.

He won the heart of audiences with his performances in films like *Baharon Ke Sapne, Aurat* (1967), *Doli, Aradhana* and *Ittefaq*.

"I like the kind of work southern heroes like Kamal Hasan, Mohanlal and Mamooty are doing since the late 80s till date. If such movies were continued to be made, I would have never chosen semi-retirement since 1996".

HITTING THE MILESTONE

With his stunning looks and impressive acting talents, he soon went on to win the heart of theater goers. He became the first superstar of Indian cinema. Such was his fan following that at midnight there would hundreds of girls waiting outside his hotel room to catch his glimpse. Girls will get themselves married to his photograph.

"I could do masala potboiler but at the same time balance it out with parallel films with simple stories. I always tried my hand at something completely out-of-the-box so script-writers, producers, directors were happy to want me".

He rocked the box office with his performances in films like *Kati Patang, Amar Prem, Shehzada, Apna Desh, Mere Jeevan Saathi, Aap Ki Kasam, Ajnabee, Namak Haraam, Maha Chor, Karm, Phir Wohi Raat, Aanchal, Kudrat, Ashanti, Agar Tum Na Hote, Awaaz, Hum Dono* and *Alag Alag*.

He gave 15 solo hits from 1969 to 1971, a record that still remains unbroken. These films include *Aradhana, Doli, Bandhan, Ittefaq, Do Raaste, Khamoshi, Safar, The Train, Kati Patang, Sachaa Jhutha, Aan Milo Sajna, Mehboob Ki Mehendi, Dushman, Anand* and *Haathi Mere Saathi*.

"These days people resort to use of abuse, vulgar scenes or use titillating tittles to make their films run. Even on my bad days I never resorted to such tactics".

His funeral procession was attended by 9 lakh people and fans came even from far-off cities like Surat, Ahmedabad, California, Singapore and other foreign countries.

> ***Success is no accident. It is hard work,***
> ***perseverance, learning, studying,***
> ***sacrifice and most of all, love of what***
> ***you are doing or learning to do.***
>
> *–Pele*

DO YOU KNOW?

Authorities in Bengal had denied giving permission of filming a shot of *Amar Prem* under the Howrah Bridge fearing that a mad rush of fans over the bridge might lead to its collapse.

A textbook prescribed by Mumbai University had a chapter named 'The Charisma of Rajesh Khanna!

> *"Even if a film flops in my career, when*
> *people say it deserved to be a hit and*
> *that I and my co-stars worked well in*
> *it and ultimately conclude saying that*
> *film is good, then that's the ultimate*
> *reward which gives me happiness".*

I am sure by now you are impressed with this first super star of Indian Cinema. He touched unprecedented heights in his career. Yet, let me share some less known stories which are not so good but can teach us some important lessons:

ONE: When I am sure by now you are impressed with this first super star of Indian Cinema. He touched unprecedented heights in his career. Yet, let me share some less known stories which are not so good but can teach us some important lessons:

TWO: When Rajesh Khanna ruled in the 1970s the nation drooled. Everyone wanted to work with the walking-talking-romancing hit machine. The mighty Gulzar came very close to working with the then-superstar Rajesh Khanna. The unknown story about the Gulzar-Khanna collaboration that never happened goes like this. Gulzar Saab and Khanna knew each other through the many films that Gulzar Saab wrote for Hrishikesh Mukherjee including Anand and Bawarchi. Gulzar Saab wanted to sign Rajesh Khanna for a romantic film which he had specially written for the Superstar. One night Rajesh Khanna called Gulzar home to his bungalow the famous Aashirwad. "Gulzar Saab who sleeps by 10 pm waited patiently till 1 am to meet the great man. But the Mighty Superstar continued drinking and cracking jokes with his durbar ignoring Gulzar Saab. He finally left in a huff, never to return again." Gulzar Saab signed Jeetendra for the same role the very next day. No matter how successful you are in your field, never ignore the people who can lift you even higher. Respect your well wishers and the people with whom you can always collaborate for bigger success.

* * *

11

A.R. Rahman

*"In all times of my life I have had a
choice of hate and love I chose love and I
am here*

Allah Rakha Rahman was born on 6 January 1967 as A.S. Dileep Kumar in Chennai in a renowned Mudaliar family, affluent for its music.

Rahman needs no introduction. He has become synonym of the Indian Film Music. The heartthrob of millions of Indian, Rahman has redefined

Indian contemporary music. He is the pride of the nation and inspiration for millions of music lovers spread across the globe.

> *"Never think that you are not like others, work hard and make sure that they are not like you"*

THE JOURNEY BEGINS

Rahman had a very tough childhood. He lost his father at the tender age of 9. His belief in God was shaken with the sudden demise of his father. The sufferings and anguish that followed after, made him a complete atheist. He never saw childhood filled with fun and games; however, responsibilities surmounted.

He made his formal debut into the world of music at the age of 11 when he joined renowned musician Illaiyaraja's troupe. Initially, he used to play keyboard but later he went on to learn guitar. He played keyboard for many television programs during his struggling days.

> *"Music is something that takes you to a world which is very different from the world of hatred, jealousy, and all those negative emotions"*

He took up music encouraged by his mother and went on to follow his father's legacy. But this, in turn, had a disastrous impact on his studies. He was driven out of many schools because of his lack of attendance.

"The search is more important than the destination"

He was part of the orchestra of M. S. Vishwanathan, Raj-Koti and Ramesh Naidu and had joined Zakir Hussain and Kunnakudi Vaidyanathan in their world tours. He made his appearance of television many a time during those days playing the keyboard on shows like Wonder Ballon telecasted on Madras Doordarshan channel. He also composed music for titbits for many Ilairaja films like K. Balachander's Punnagai Mannan.

"All my life I have had a choice of hate and love. I chose love and I am here"

HITTING THE MILESTONE

All the success and honors Rahman has achieved in these many years have not changed him as a person. He continues to be humble, modest and a down to earth human being who is still shy and devout in his nature. An introvert, his phenomenal work does all the talking on his behalf. Staying out of controversies and

saving his energies for his incredible compositions, Rahman's life is summed best in the words of his favorite prayer "O

God, if I worship thee for fear of hell, burn me in hell, and if I worship thee in hope of Paradise, exclude me from Paradise, but if I worship thee for thy own sake, grudge me not thy everlasting beauty."

> ***"Great people do not believe in making right decisions. They make decisions first and then make them right."***
>
> **–Ratan Tata**

Rahman has taken Indian film music to a new platform with Andrew Lloyd Weber's Bombay Dreams. His contribution towards music and Indian film industry is unmatched and enlightened life of many with the power of his soul-touching melodies. Winner of infinite awards including the Academy Awards, Rahman's glory will hopefully continue to touch new heights in the years to come.

Do you know?

Rahman's life has been filled with struggle and hardship. Everything he has achieved today is because of his sheer dedication and passion for music. He lost his father at the age of 9 to a mysterious illness which was believed by a few to be black magic performed by his rivals.

A high school dropout, Rahman started supporting his family since the age of 11.

Today, Mr. Rahman is a brand in himself. He is not only respected and revered by millions of his fans for his talent but also for humanness. Even today, Mr. Rahman doesn't work on his own convenience instead he is considerate. In the research on his life, I have found a very unique quality of this music sensation – HE IS ALWAYS CONSIDERATE FOR OTHER PEOPLE'S CONVENIENCE.

This Oscar winner likes and is habitual of working through the night and he accepts it's much more convenient for him to record in the nights. Yet, he shown flexibility by agreeing to Alka Yagnik's comfort of recording in the early morning for *Mehendi Hai Rachnewali* from *Zubeidaa* and *Mitawa* from *Lagaan*.

Ms Lata Mangeshkar is also a day person and Mr Rahman has teamed up with her as well and recorded for her in the day time. If you are considerate to people, the universe becomes considerate to you. Let me tell you yet another revelation about universe being considerate. AR Rahman Wasn't Danny Boyle's First Choice For *Slumdog Millionaire*. Mr Boyle first thought about Jack White to compose the music for the epic movie. Yet, on repeated recommendation from one of his crew members that he must meet Mr. Rahman. Boyle decided to meet the star and the rest all is history. AR Rahman's *'Jai Ho'* song not only became super hit but one of his all time greats, fetching him the Oscar.

Just think about it .. all because someone selflessly recommended Rahman to Boyle.

"AR Rahman's talent is matched by his appetite, his modesty and his generosity." Says Denny Boyle.

Be Nice To People.

* * *

12

Rajinikanth

I was a conductor, today I'm a star.

Rajinikanth was born on 12 December, 1950 in Bangalore province of the princely state of Mysore, in the present-day Karnataka in a Maharastrian Rajput family. He was named Shivaji Rao Gaikwad by his parents Jijabai and Ramoji Rao Gaekwad. He was the youngest of his four siblings.

"Life is about learning, and it is never too late to learn"

***If you think that you are too old to learn then
you should think that you are too old to live***

–Dinesh Verma

THE JOURNEY BEGINS

Rajnikanth began his acting career on stage. He was offered

roles for mythological moral plays by the notable Kannada playwright and director *Topi Muniappa*. His most remarkable performance was the portrayal of *Duryodhana*. He was motivated to join the Madras Film Institute by his friend Raj Bahadur who also assisted him financially all through the two years he spent there, learning the titbits of acting.

During one of the plays on stage, his acting caught the attention of director K. Balachander. Rajnikanth began learning Tamil on Balanchander's advice, a skill that helped him all through his career.

"Yesterday I was a conductor, today I'm a star, tomorrow what I'll be only He knows!"

Initially he played the antagonist in Tamil films but later on went on to grab substantial roles as an actor. In a short span he was proclaimed as the superstar of Tamil cinema and continues to be idolized in the popular south Indian culture of India.

HITTING THE MILESTONE

Rajnikanth is still revered as the 'demigod' and is honored as a deity in many parts of the southern India. There are many temples dedicated to him and is considered as one of the most influential actor of Indian cinema. Even after receiving numerous recognitions and honors on Indian and International platforms, he still continues to remain humble and down to earth.

> *You won't get anything without hard work. What you get without hard work will never fructify.*
>
> *– Rajinikanth*

DO YOU KNOW?

After the death of his mother at the age of 5, he struggled with an impoverished lifestyle during his childhood. During that time, he often did odd jobs as a coolie in his community. He attended the Government Model Primary School at Gavipuram, Bangalore, where he had his elementary education in Kannada.

Between 1966 and 1973 he worked in many places in Chennai and Bangalore. He performed various jobs before joining the then Bangalore Transport Service as a bus conductor in Bangalore.

> ***"Don't wait until everything is just***
> ***right. It will never be perfect. There will***
> ***always be challenges, obstacles and less***
> ***than perfect conditions. So what. Get***
> ***started now. With each step you take,***
> ***you will grow stronger and stronger,***
> ***more and more skilled, more and more***
> ***self-confident and more and more***
> ***successful".***

Rajnikanth is perhaps one of the very few stars in Indian Cinema who has really come from a humble beginning and became a star as a result of his own struggles and learning along the journey. It won't be wrong if I claim that he is the most famous ever actor from regional films in India.

Rajnikanth started his journey of success very early from many odd jobs including the one most talked about as conductor in Bangalore Bus Transport Service. If you closely look at his life, you will understand the cornerstones of this life of epic success and inspiration. Let me present four of the lessons from his life to you:

1. Start wherever you can, utilize whatever talent or resources you have, do things, get feedback, learn, execute again and keep growing.

2. We as human beings tend to look at the roses but try to look below and behind. Every rose blossomed on and above the thorns. He had his share of failures where he put in everything he had in movies which bombed causing him unimaginable losses. But this god of

South Indian movies knows how to turn every failure into stepping stone and jump to the next stone which can even be a milestone of success. Learn to work hard and irrespective of failure or success move on.

3. Rajnikanth is a rare actor who is literally worshipped by his millions of followers in India and abroad. His fans have built temples to worship for his prosperity and health. Yet, he is very humble. He always gives credit of his success to others and has the guts to accept the blame and criticism of anything which fails. Despite his enormous success as a star, as a person, he has stayed a simple, accessible, respectful, dignified person like he has always been. He has never let success change him as a person.

4. When you are so successful – rights to give suggestions and advices come naturally to you. Yet, success never went to the head of this star. Rajinikanth is famous for not interfering in others' work, be it the writer or the cameraman or the director. Once the team is in place, he fully trusts them with their processes and just gives to whatever is asked of him. No interfering of anyone's task but whatever is given to him – he will put his heart and soul to finish it in such a way that no one else can do it better.

* * *

Madhuri Dixit

*I wanted to make a name, which
I have done.*

Madhuri Dixit was born on 15 May, 1967 in Mumbai. She is one of the few actresses of Hindi cinema who had the charisma of taking a film to success without any of the strong actor presence. Smitten by her stunning looks, Madhuri was the inspiration behind many paintings of M.F. Hussain. An acclaimed dancer, she has the aura of setting the screen on fire with her impressive dancing moves, astonishing beauty and electrifying performances.

> *"I have never bothered to find out who the other heroine is in my film at any stage of my career. Competition doesn't matter because I give my best to all my shots anyway"*

A trained Kathak dancer, Madhuri did her graduation from the Parle College Mumbai and aspired a career in microbiology.

THE STRUGGLE BEGINS

Madhuri made her debut to the silver screen in 1984 with *Abodh*. Her next few releases failed to create a buzz in the industry. It took her close to three years for making a mark in Bollywood for herself. *Tezaab* was the film that brought her to the spotlight and gave her the credit that was due. This was also the beginning of her hit paring opposite Anil Kapoor. They gave back to back hits like *Ram Lakhan, Prem Prathiyaga, Tridev*, and *Parinda,* that was India's official entry in Oscars that year.

> *"When I joined films I was clear I wanted to make a name, which I have done"*

HITTING THE MILESTONE

Madhuri gave one of her most remembered performances in Indra Kumar's *Dil* in 1990. She was paired opposite Aamir

Khan in the movie and won the Filmfare Best Actress Award. In the year 1991, *Saajan* starring Madhuri, Salman and Sanjay did a good business in the box-office. She starred yet again opposite Anil Kapoor in films like *Khel, Zindagi Ek Jua*, and *Beta*. She appeared in one of her most remarkable dance sequences, *Dhak dhak karne laga...* in *Beta* and since then has been coined by media as the 'Dhak Dhak girl'.

> *"I feel I am capable of much more. I guess every artist feels that way. If you are satisfied, you begin to stagnate"*

Her role in Subhash Ghai's *Khalnayak* created widespread sensation. Also starring Jackie Shroff and Sanjay Dutt, the movie was a blockbuster. She was appreciated for her role as Ganga and the song sequence *Choli ke peeche kya hai...* Her next release with the Rajshri production and Suraj Barajatiya directorial *Hum Apke Hain Kaun* was a record- breaking hit. Her portrayal of Nisha opposite Salman Khan won her the third Filmfare Best Actress Award. Her next releases were *Raja* and *Yaarana* in 1995.

> *I try to give my best to everything I do. I don't think of housework as beneath my dignity; that's just the way I was brought up.*
>
> *–Madhuri Dixit*

She was part of Yash Chopra's *Dil To Pagal Hain* in 1997 and in 2000 paired again with Anil Kapoor for Rajkumar Santoshi's *Pukar.* She played the protagonist in M.F. Hussain's

Gaj Gamini. Hussain made the movie inspired by her and it covered many aspects of a woman's life.

In 2001, she played Janaki in *Lajja* and the following year she rocked the theatres with her role as Chandramukhi in Sanjay Leela Bhansali's *Devdas*. She won the Filmfare Best Supporting Actress Award for her smashing performance.

"For me dancing is not just moving your arms and legs but basically it's a very spiritual experience. It's part of me and a second nature to me. You can say it is in my blood"

Post her marriage to surgeon Dr. Shriram Madhav Nene in 1999 she took a sabbatical for five years. The couple has two children and has moved back to India from the U.S. As she made her comeback in Bollywood with *Aaja Nachle* in 2007. Her post-marriage films have been *Dedh Ishqiya* and *Gulaab Gang* based on the life activist Sampat Kumar.

She was honored with the second-highest civilian award in India, the Padma Shri by the Government of India in 2008.

Do you know?

An accomplished dancer, Madhuri Dixit learnt Kathak for eight years. She didn't intend to join Bollywood but was considering a career in microbiology.

> *"When you live for a strong purpose, then hard work isn't an option. It's a necessity"*.

Madhuri Dixit who is also known as dhak dhak girl is undisputed queen of dance in Bollywood. How did she manage to become the queen of dance in India where almost every girl or boy loves moving legs on any song.

The answer to this question is CONSISTENT PRACTICE.

Find your passion and decide to become the best in whatever you love to do. Madhuri had so many likings as a teenage girl but she zeroed down to ONE THING where she wanted to make a name for herself and that was DANCE.

Once she decided on one thing. She dedicated herself to the practice of dance with a discipline of a world class athlete.

रियाज़ बहुत जरूरी है।

—माधुरी दीक्षित नेने

Like it's said "Don't practice until you get it right. Practice until you can't get it wrong." Always remember that repetition is key to perfection. When you practice, you use your skills and you build on them. Small amounts of daily practice would give you exponential results and help you remember steps and improve your technique. Daily practice helps you build confidence, endurance, and bring quality to your art. Make a daily schedule and devote a few hours to your passion. Try and record what you are doing so that you can review it later and perfect your steps.

"You have to practice consistently every day"

– Madhuri Dixit Nene

Everything that has value in life is a product of consistency. Success, health, fitness, wealth, passion, friendships, relationships, and all other aspirations are all about consistency. Similarly, in dance, consistency is very important. Even studies show that 80% of everything new that we learnt is forgotten.

Go find your passion and devote yourself in pursuit of perfection.

* * *

14

Sanjay Dutt

The most important thing is to be a human being.

Born on 29 July 1959, Sanjay is a 58 years old film star from Mumbai, Maharashtra. He has done his schooling from The Lawrence School, Sanawar (Near Kasauli, Himachal Pradesh). Sanjay Dutt has led a very unusual life. Along with fame and fortune which were gifted to him at birth, he has also had many setbacks in his personal life as well as his career.

***Fame and fortune are as hard to
find as a lightning strike.***

–P. N. Elrod

Sanjay Dutt is the star son of two of the biggest names in Hindi Cinema of their era, Sunil and Nargis Dutt. Very few people know that Sanjay stared as a child actor in one of his father Sunil Dutt's film titled Reshma Aur Shera.

*"As a person, I'm pretty much the same
except that I've come to terms with who
my real friends and supporters are. I
don't get particularly friendly with new
people at first go"*

Sanjay was to make his official and formal debut in films. Sanjay coming from a filmi background with two talented actors as his parents, naturally there were too much pressure and expectations from him.

A few weeks before Sanjay's debut film *Rocky* released, he lost his mother to the dreaded illness of cancer. Sanjay was devastated, but his father too was by his grief and hence could not provide the emotional anchor that he so badly needed. His film *Rocky* (1981) was a moderate success.

In 1982, Sanjay gave another hit with *Vidhaata*. However Sanjay's personal life took a turn for the worse and he began to lead a life filled with booze, parties and drugs.

*"I would advise all the people to never
do things in excesses it will not only
murky your own future but also all
your loved ones would suffer too and
steer away from drugs and alcohol"*

His drug addiction began to affect his career too. Sanjay was being considered for the film Hero, but later Subhash Ghai opted not to cast him due to his habit of drug addiction.

After his bail, Sanjay's case in the 1993 bomb blasts had been on for the last 14 years. During this period, the actor was made to do many rounds of court houses. Sanjay was also living in constant angst and fear of having to go back to jail. Finally, on 31 July 2007 Sanjay Dutt's fears became a reality and he was sentenced to six years imprisonment for his role in the 1993 bomb blasts case. Sanjay this time, however, tried to take his situation in his stride; he kept up a brave face and was supported by the entire film industry, his family and his loved ones. Sanjay spent two separate stints in jail before he was finally released on bail.

*"Twenty years from now you will be
more disappointed by the things that you
didn't do than by the ones you did do."*

–Mark Twain

DID YOU KNOW?

The media was ruthless and kept printing stories of how his mother Nargis's ill health had worsened due to her son's drug addiction. They also criticized him as an actor. Sanjay, who was already in knee-deep depression, was further pushed in addiction. His father Sunil Dutt decided to intervene and tried his best to pull his son out of the darkness. Sunil Dutt sent Sanjay to a drug rehabilitation centre in America. Sanjay stayed there and recuperated for several months in the rehab centre and through sheer effort, successfully kicked off his drug addiction.

But after that Sanjay got into bad company, he began associating with the underworld. And in the year 1993 faced another blow when he was arrested in April, 1993 on charges of keeping illegal weapons that were provided to him by the alleged Bombay bomb blast mastermind and mafia don Abu Salem. He spent more than 18 months in Jail. During this time he received huge support from friends, family, Bollywood film fraternity and millions of fans from all over the world. He also received emotional strength from his then girlfriend, model Rhea Pillai. His father, Sunil Dutt was into politics and had a lot of goodwill amongst influential people. After 18 months, he was finally able to get his son out on bail. Sunil Dutt again came to the rescue of his son. After he was released on bail, Sanjay was indeed a changed man.

He has worked in many movies, after that, and most of them have been very successful. He has given unforgettable performance in '*Munnabhai series*'.

He is an actor, who has his fans across all generations, from small kids to the old generation.

He is the best example, where we can say that life gives a second chance. He grabbed the opportunities again, and has ever since become exemplary.

> *Life's up and downs provide windows of opportunity to determine your values and goals. Think of using all obstacles as stepping stones to build the life you want.*

Hailing from a Bollywood family and also having a massive political connect; the life of Sanjay Dutt has always been under scrutiny. Not surprisingly, this good boy turned bad with drugs, illegal possession of arms and ammunition and such charges being pressed against him. Every Bollywood buff knows about the scandals, love life and the controversial details of Sanjay Dutt's life. I feel that we can learn a lot from his good and bad deeds or habits. Let me share few of those:

1. Beware of the kind of company you live in. Good company will make you good and the bad company will do its magic too. You become the kind of person you spend your time with. Sanjay Dutt has been into so many problems because of his connections with wrong people.

2. Own your mistakes: No matter how careful you are, mistakes will happen in life. Small or big – just own those, accept those, commit not to repeat, apologize

and move on. Sanjay Dutt once said "I am a human being and I made mistakes and I should be honest about it."

3.   Leave the past behind and focus on the present. This is how this actor still keeps on doing some of the best movies of Bollywood. He knows how to let go the past and embrace the present.

4.   This one from the silver screen. Indeed, there are so many things which can be learned from his dialogues in movies yet the best one is *'jaadu ki jhappi'*. In the movie *'Munnabhai MBBS'* which means let's not brood over past. Leave the rant and hug it over.

✳ ✳ ✳

15

Hrithik Roshan

Born to actor Rakesh and his wife Pinky Roshan, Hrithik had Bollywood in his genes. Born to a filmi family on 10 January, 1974 in Mumbai, Hritihik started making appearance in films since his childhood days.

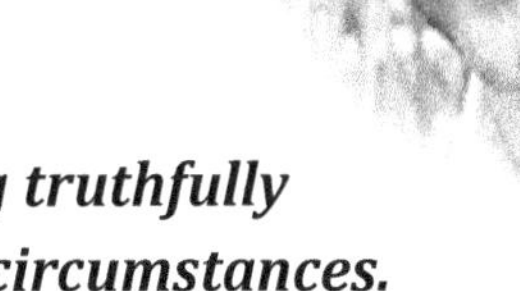

Acting is behaving truthfully under imaginary circumstances.

–Sanford Meisner

THE JOURNEY BEGINS

Coming from the family of filmmakers, Bollywood entry was expected to be swift but that wasn't the case for him. Hrithik spent initial years behind the camera learning the first lessons. He had spent hours in gym to get a perfectly toned body. He had severe speech disorder for which he still undergoes therapies. Then there was his sixth finger which

he had to keep away from the camera. He learnt dancing and Urdu before stepping into Bollywood.

He made his debut as an actor in 2000 with Rakesh Rohan's *Kaho Na Pyar Hai.* Hritihk with his smashing performance in the film went on to receive Filmfare best debutant and the Best Actor Award.

In 2001 he appeared in Karan Johar's *Kabhie Khushi Kabhi Gham* that also starred Amitabh Bacchhan, Shahrukh Khan, Kajol and Kareena Kapoor. The movie went on to become a big commercial success and India's highest-grossing film in the overseas market.

"I am glad I have the intelligence to understand what is happening to me. If I allow myself to get affected by all this hype, I'll stunt my growth as an actor and be damned for life. I know that I still have a long way to go before I can even aspire to equal the achievements of any of the superstars. I know I am good at my job, and I am sure I will be damn good one day but right now, I also know how bad I can be."

HITTING THE MILESTONE

The father-son duo again created wonders with *Koi Mil Gaya.* The movie about an alien not only went on to become an overnight blockbuster but has been one of the most successful films in Hindi cinema. The next sequels of the films that followed also went on to create a new record for Bollywood. He received his third Filmfare Best Actor Award for his spectacular performance in *Dhoom 2*. His performance was widely appreciated for the epic saga *Jodha Akbar* and received his first international honor at the Golden Minbar International Film Festival. The success and recognitions received so far has established Hritihik as one of the most popular and sought after stars of Hindi cinema.

"Every once a week, I get up and feel that I cannot act anymore. I just get very unsure of myself. But, once I give my first shot, I'm back on track. Insecurity isn't bad, it makes me work harder."

Hrithik has been hailed infinite times for his incredible dancing talent. Revered as the Greek God by the Indian media, the Jr. Roshan is known for his versatility and professionalism.

***The best acting is instinctive. It's not intellectual,
it's not mechanical, it's instinctive.***

–Craig MacDonald

There came a point in his career when he was written off by the critics but he didn't let it go and today he is regarded as one of the most successful contemporary stars in Bollywood.

Do you know?

Hrithik has been suffering from a stuttering problem since he was 6 and had to undergo several painful speech therapy sessions to overcome the problem. Hrithik continues those sessions still today as he is paranoid about his stuttering problem and incoherent speech disorders to come back.

*"Trust yourself. Create the kind of self
that you will be happy to live with all
your life. Make the most of yourself
by fanning the tiny, inner sparks of
possibility into flames of achievement".*

Diamonds that shine don't attain near perfection early on. Metamorphosis is time consuming, exactly like how grape is turned into wine, people take time to shine. Hrithik Roshan, the heart throb of the nation was not born perfect, he too underwent severe adversities. It is a common assumption that children of Stars or Celebrities tend to enjoy affluent lives, but it isn't true.

As a child Hrithik faced severe stuttering issues. He had to live with his mates talk fluently around him, while he had to compose himself with an almighty strength to utter syllables. For a kid who finds expressing through words as his worst nightmare, it is a heart breaking experience.

"For oral tests at school, I used to bunk school, I used to fall sick, I used to break my hand, I used to get a sprain." (Bollywood star talks about his stuttering, n.d.)

In one of his interviews he mentioned he had practiced for 36 hours to be able to tell his cook what to make for the dinner. This might sound unreal, it isn't.

Then he got affected with body shaming because of his double thumb in a hand and had to hide that while talking. On one hand people use their hand gestures to score some brownie points while speaking but this gentleman had to hide.

Hrithik, at the age of 21 was diagnosed with Scoliosis-Curved Spinal Cord, and was suggested not to take up acting as a profession, as it demanded a lot of physical strain on the Spine, which might put him in a wheelchair for life.

Misfortune struck the actor again in 2010. He was diagnosed with a bad knee, apparently the condition made his left knee incredibly brittle, even worse than old people. The doctors feared the knee lasting not more than a year. In July of 2013, a blood clot was spotted in his brain. He had to get under the knife, which has infinitesimal chances of recovery. In fact, the procedure was so risky that the chances of death were higher.

Yet another personal setback – In 2014 December he got separated with his 13 year wife Sussanne Khan. This definitely would not have been easy for the doting husband and a dad to two handsome kids.

What is there in the whole story for us to learn?

A LOT.

We may not have been blessed with similar family background and may have been blessed with perfect speech. But we all have our own fears. Just identify those and face those. Look for daily improvement through daily action. Embrace the struggles and come out as a champion. DO WHATEVER BUT KEEP PUSHING YOURSELF EVERYDAY. HAVE THE MINDSET OF A WINNER AND GO FOR YOUR DREAMS.

Just imagine if you have a car and know how to drive, would you drive only when the road is perfect? Not really. The road will have speed breakers, it will have potholes and there will be red signals which will make you wait, of course you may come across heavy traffic jams.

Then why don't you go for your dreams! Make Hrithik Roshan your consistent reference for all the motivation you need; get start and keep moving.

* * *

Amrish Puri

I am happy to play the bad man

Amrish Puri, Indian movies actor born on 22 June 1932 in Nawanshahr, in the district of Jalandhar, Punjab. He was fourth among the five children born to Sri Nihal Puri and Ved Kaur. He was the first cousin of the actor and singer K.L. Saigal. His elder brothers Chaman and Madan Puri were both established actors of Hindi Cinema and had an elder sister Chandrakanta and a younger brother Harish Puri.

THE JOURNEY BEGINS

Amrish Puri spent most of his childhood in Nawanshahr and later moved to Shimla, Himachal Pradesh for pursuing graduation from B.M. College. He came to Mumbai following the footsteps of his elder brothers. Madan was by now one of the renowned names in the film industry having played parts in many successful films.

"I am happy to play the bad man"

HITTING THE MILESTONE

Apart from Hindi cinema, Amrish has done movies in Kannada, Punjabi, Malayalam, Telegu, Tamil and even

some Hollywood films. But his most remarkable contribution has been towards Hindi Cinema. He made his Hollywood debut with Steven Spielberg's Indiana Jones and the Temple of Doom where he played the antagonist Mola Ram. He has enacted in over four hundred films. His impressive screen presence went on to secure dominating roles for him making him stand out amongst the other villains of the day. He became the Mogambo of Bollywood after Shekhar Kapur's 1987 blockbuster, Mr. India where he played the role of Mogambo. People still remember him for that role.

Amrish Puri, the man who exemplified terror, petrified people with horror and personified evil used to put in every character he portrayed on screen. With this ability to get into the depth of any character he played, audiences got the glimpse of a true hero in him. The list of his hit films include *Meri Jung* (1985), *Nagina* (1986), *Mr India*(1987), *Ram Lakhan* (1989), *Ghayal* (1990), *Saudagar*(1991), *Deewana* (1992), *Tahalka* (1992), *Damini* (1993), *Karan Arjun*(1995), *Ghatak* (1996), *Karan Koyla* (1997), *Pardes* (1997), *Taal* (1999), *Badshah* (1999), *Nayak: The Real Hero*(2001), *Dilwale Dulhaniya Le Jayenge* (1995), *Gadar: Ek Prem Katha*(2001), *Aitraz* (2004), *Lakshya* (2004), *Garv* (2004) and *Mujhse Shaadi Karogi* (2004).

Do you know?

Amrish Puri after failing in his first screen test decided to settle down in his job with Employees' State Insurance Corporation. It was at the same time that he began his stage career with appearance in plays written by Satyadev Dubey. After a few performances, he became an accomplished artist on stage and went on to win the prestigious Sangeet Natak Academy Award in 1979. The admiration he got from theatre helped him give impressive performance on television. Eventually. he could make entry ino the Indian Film Industry.

Failure is only the opportunity to
begin again, more intelligently.

–Henry Ford

The charismatic screen presence of Amrish Puri had overshadowed the main leads in many of his movies. The antithesis and the obvious climax seemed to be a sarcasm as screen presence had already been dominated by Amrish Puri.

Being a leader gives you charisma. If you look and study the leaders who have succeeded, that's where charisma comes from, from the leading.

–Seth Godin

"There are two types of people who will tell you that you cannot make a difference in this world: those who are afraid to try and those who are afraid you will succeed."

He was an actor, who for over 30 years and beyond, has shocked, frightened, and inspired generations to embrace negative roles with refreshing appreciation and positive message, setting a benchmark for the future.

If you go deep inside his life you will find that he had passion for acting and discipline for life. He started his Bollywood journey at the age of 40 years but before that he used to be an insurance agent where he travelled to far off areas on his bike and practiced theatre between his days.

I feel compelled to present these four big lessons from his silver screen presence:

1. **Aitraaz (2004)-** आदमी के पास दिमाग हो तो वो अपना दर्द भी बेच सकता है। In this dialogue, he told that if a person is

able to become a good salesperson by applying his or her mind, he/she can even sell his/her pains.

2. **Dilwale Dulhaniya Le Jayenge (1995)-** जा सिमरन जी ले अपनी ज़िंदगी *Dilwale Dulhania Le Jayenge* was one of the greatest movies ever made. This movie had Amrish Puri in a very pivotal role. He was the father of Simran (Kajol), who loved Raj (Shahrukh), and he stopped their union.

   In the end, Amrish Puri finally allowed Simran to get married to Raj, and this has so much depth in itself.

   We should never be obsessive about people doing what you want them to do. Let they be happy, it's their life.

3. **Deewana (1992)** - ये दौलत भी क्या चीज़ है जिसके पास जितनी भी आती है कम ही लगती है। Amrish Puri played the role of a greedy uncle named Dheerendra Pratap. In the end, while submerged in alcohol, he admitted that money has no depth and greed has no fulfillment.

   He emotionally told that wealth has no meaning in life and no matter how rich people become, money will always lure them.

4. **Mr. India (1987)** - मोगैम्बो खुश हुआ। Today the organizations spend so much of money for finding some great tag lines. This was a great tag line in the movie. Here Amrish Puri had the goal of conquering entire India and he kept on repeating this to all his team mates in all his meetings. Even after making a great tag line the organizations need to spend money,

energy and time to take it to the people so that they start connecting with this and this becomes their natural response for the organization/brand. KNOW WHAT YOU WANT AND LET YOUR PEOPLE ALSO KNOW THE SAME.

Anil Kapoor

I love acting so much that the feeling
transfers on screen

Anil Kapoor was born on 24 December, 1956 in Mumbai, Surinder and Nirmal Kapoor. The renowned producer and director Boney Kapoor is his elder brother and actor Sanjay Kapoor is his younger sibling. They have a sister named Reena. His father was working as the secretary of Shammi Kapoor and the family spent their initial years in a Chawl in Tilak Nagar, Mumbai.

Acting is not about being someone different.
It's finding the similarity in what is apparently
different, then finding myself in there.

–Meryl Streep

Anil was a recluse in his early childhood days and attended Our Lady of Perpetual Succor School. As a child, he was driven by the Bollywood films and enjoyed the ones that he got to see during the Ganesh Maha Utsav celebrations in his locality. A fan of the legendary showman Raj Kapoor, his acting too got influenced by the Kapoor scion. He played the child in Sashi Kapoor starrer Tu Payal Main Geet but unfortunately the film was never released.

"Instead of focusing on my looks I focus
on the character"

THE JOURNEY BEGINS

After completing his schooling, Anil went on to study in St. Xaviers College, Mumbai. Here he was introduced with Mazhar Khan and the meeting inspired him to join Rosha Taneja's acting school.

"I still feel like a young kid on his first date, every time I enter the studio, I feel as charged up as ever. Perhaps the truth is simply that I love acting so much that the feeling transfers itself on screen."

He made his silver screen debut as a character artist in Hamare Tumhare. Nasiruddin Shah starrer *Wo 7 Din* was the first film that had Anil Kapoor as the male lead. His powerful performance in the film was widely noticed and there was no looking back for the star from there.

HITTING THE MILESTONE

Anil has acted in over 100 movies so far and has several other pipelined in the production stage. As a producer, he has given Hindi cinema movies like Gandhi My Father and *Badhaai Ho Badhaai*. He has also been the Casting Director/Outdoor In-charge of Hum Paanch.

> *"But it is not a conscious strategy to go for unconventional roles"*

Kapoor made his Hollywood debut with the Academy Award-winning Danny Boyle's *Slumdog Millionare*. He shared the Screen Actor Guild Award for Outstanding Performance by a Cast in a Motion Picture. He impressed the American press globally with his performance in the eighth season of 24. He came up with the Hindi version of the widely popular series 24 that generated rave reviews.

DO YOU KNOW?

During his struggling days, Anil Kapoor used to commute by bus and train to Chembur and Bombay VT and then used to walk rest of the way to save money.

He was thrown out of college in his second year for lack of attendance. His dream to join the reputed Pune Film Institute was broken after he failed in the written test.

Undoubtedly education is important, but what is more important is life skills and values.

–Dinesh Verma

"One important key to success is self-confidence. An important key to self-confidence is preparation".

There is a lot to learn from this legend who has been around for almost 4 decades yet is considered as one of the coolest actors in the industry. Let me present 5 of his top quotes which can be constant source of inspiration to be fit & hit in life:

"You have to have that madness. You have to have that self belief because there will always be people around to de-motivate."

"One should go by the script not by number of heroes a film has. I had no issues in working for films which had multiple heroes."

"Nobody rallies around you. You will have to help yourself in bad & down times."

Anil Kapoor

*"I invest in people, why should I fire them.
My hairstylist and driver have been with
me even before my daughter, Sonam was
born. I don't believe in hire & fire."*

*"I have never had any doubts in myself.
I was always confident from within
and the reason for that is I really work
hard on everything I get onto."*

* * *

*"I invest in people, why should I fire them.
My hairstylist and driver have been with
me even before my daughter, Sonam was
born. I don't believe in hire & fire."*

18

Govinda

I believe in miracles.

Govinda was born to actor Arun Ahuja and Nirmala Devi on 21 December, 1963 in Mumbai. A fabulous actor and a great dancer, Govinda has made appearance in over 120 Hindi films. Winner of numerous awards, Govinda has also represented Mumbai North constituency in the Lower House of Indian Parliament.

> *"I'm not keen on offbeat films for
> creative satisfaction. I want to do them
> to win awards. And that's the honest
> truth"*

THE JOURNEY BEGINS

His actor father and classical singer mother had lived in a bungalow in the Mumbai's Carter Road during the initial days of their marriage. His father had invested all his earnings in a movie that he produced. The movie failed miserably in the box-office and so was Arun Ahuja's health. They lost almost everything they had and moved to Virar.

He made his Bollywood debut with *Tan Badan* directed by his uncle Anand. He was paired opposite Neelam for many of his films and the duo delivered hit like *Love 86* (1986), *Khudgarz* (1987).

Govinda has carved a niche for himself in the Film industry with his blockbuster movies like *Shola Aur Shabnam, Aankhen, Coolie No. 1, Haseena Maan Jaayegi* and *Partner*.

> *"You have to work hard and not think
> about failure and successes. That is
> everywhere"*

HITTING THE MILESTONE

In June 1999 BBC New Online Users had voted Govinda as the tenth greatest star of stage and screen in the last thousand years. Govinda's pairing along with ace director David

Dhawan has produced many hits. The actor has received widespread acclaim from critics as well as audiences for his comedy timing and caliber to dance with an ease.

"I believe in miracles. That I'm a successful actor is the biggest of them all."

Do you know?

Govinda is the youngest of his 6 siblings and spent his childhood days in Virar living a tough life.

Govinda met his wife Sunita at the time of his struggle. The two fell in love and got married but the news was not made public for a long time as Govinda feared that it will have a negative effect on his career.

All of us start from zero. We take the right decision and become a hero.

–Govinda

Govinda has been a man of less words and more action. This actor has always been one of the most entertaining actors through his simple yet pleasing dance moves as well as his comic sense. He believes in the blessings of parents, teachers and almighty. He has spoken at many events with lot of emotions about his mother being his role model and the best teacher who shaped his values for life.

Govinda puts serving parents above anything else including the degrees & certificates.

He also believes in the power of concentrating on ONE THING. An actor has to do many things to manage his/her career including relationships with co-stars and the whole eco system of film-industry as the other revenue producing activities like advertisements and appearance in public events. Yet, for Govinda all other activities have been secondary other than core acting. Be it his comic sense or dance or his appearance on TV and other non-screen events – all have been managed keeping his acting at the center. We must find our main thing and stay focused around.

> **"The main thing is to keep the
> main thing, the main thing."**
>
> **– Stephen Covey**

* * *

19

Irrfan Khan

"A nation needs to know how to utilise talent".

I rrfan Khan was born on 7 January, 1967 in a traditional Muslim family. He was born in Jaipur where his father owned a tyre business. It was while pursuing his degree of M.A. in 1984 that Irrfan earned a scholarship for the prestigious National School of Drama.

"I can't think of a more pathetic situation for an actor than to do a film

**and not connect to it. And I pray to God
that I never face that situation".**

THE STRUGGLE BEGINS

Irrfan made his acting debut in television. He had been a part of many shows in Doordarshan like *Chanakya, Bharat Ek Khoj, Sara Jahan Hamara, Banegi Apni Baat, Chandrakanta* and *AnooGoonj*.

***I had always been feeling uncomfortable
in my mind about giving advice to others
and not acting upon it myself.***

–Lal Bahadur Shastri

HITTING THE MILESTONE

He made his debut on the silver screen in 1990. His career in the film industry failed to flourish because his initial movies didn't do well at the box-office. It was after Asif Kapadia cast him in his movie. He soon became an international face. He was critically acclaimed for his appearance in films like *Maqbool, Rog, Haasil*.

**"A nation needs to know how to utilise
talent"**

His roles in international projects like A Mighty Heart and The Darjeeling Limited were widely appreciated. He was also part of the academy award-winning film Slumdog Millionaire.

His latest movies have been New York, I Love You and

Paan Singh Tomar. He entertained audiences worldwide with his roles in In Treatment, The Amazing Spider-Man, Life of Pi. He has been cast as an antagonist in 2015 release Jurassic World.

"A film engages you emotionally and intellectually"

Do You Know?

Irrfan Khan till today reads at least one script of a Hollywood movie in a week. He keeps himself prepared and does his homework well. He stays awake till 3 in night, makes notes and spends time to understand his role and character.

He asked for 11 rewrites for directing an episode of *Banegi Apni Baat* from his writer wife. To understand the character better, he had once taken his wife Sutapa to a police station in Mumbai. It is his indulgence in his role that makes him create indelible impression in the minds of the cinema lovers.

"What happens with every role, you have to trick yourself, you have to creatively find ways to explore the mental state of your character".

When life hits you hard – you can either suffer & crib or live a joyful life and teach lessons to the world. Indeed, this can be your opportunity to become inspirational. Ah, this of course needs you to have some real strong spine. Irrfan, has chosen the later. He has millions of fans and even after being diagnosed with cancer he never let them down. In fact, the fans have become even more proud of their super star because of the way he handled the dangerous disease. Here is a set of three awesome life lessons from Irrfan himself in his own words:

ONE: UNCERTAINTY IS THE ONLY CERTAINTY

"Life is uncertain. I don't have a crystal ball and I don't know what's going to happen today, tomorrow or the next day. No one does. We can enjoy our present moment, making the most of our lives or we can worry about what might or might not happen. While there are a lot of things I can't influence – I can actively control my attitude and how I react to any given situation. It takes a lot to rattle me now and I don't get easily worked up about things that are beyond my control."

TWO: DON'T BE ANXIOUS ABOUT DEATH

"My mind could always tell me to hang a kind of chip on my neck and say 'I have this disease and I could die in a few months or a year or two. Or I could just avoid this conversation completely and live my life the way it offers me. And it offers me so much. I admit, I was walking around with blinders. I couldn't see what it offered me."

THREE: LEARN TO ACCEPT WHAT LIFE GIVES YOU

"There are challenges which life throws at you. But I have started believing in the way this condition has tested me, really, really tested me in all the aspects – physical, emotional, spiritual. It has put me in a rapture state. Initially, I was shaken. I didn't know. I was very, very vulnerable. But slowly, there was another way to look at things that is much more powerful, productive & healthy. I just want people to believe that nature is much more trustworthy and one must trust that."

FOUR: UNEXPECTED THINGS CAN COME AT ANYTIME

"My days are unpredictable, I don't plan. I go for breakfast and then I don't have a plan. I take things as they come. That has really been helping me a lot. I don't make plans. I am just spontaneous. And I am loving this experience. I know because we are living in a world that is packed with plans, it sounds unrealistic. How could you live your life like that? But life is so mysterious and has so much to offer, we don't really try things. I am trying and I'm loving it. I am in a really fortunate state."

Johnny Lever

*We are all gifted in some way
or the other*

The comedy king of India Johnny Lever was born as John Prakasa Rao on 14 August, 1957 in Janumala in Prakasam, Andhra Pradesh. His parents were Prakash Rao Janumala and Karunamma Janumala and belongs to Telegu Christian community. He could study only till 7th grade as the financial condition of the family couldn't afford it after that.

*Making people emotional is the easiest thing
that you can do. You just have to tell how
unprivileged was your family, how cruel were
your circumstances and you will see misty
eyes. But, what really needs acting marvel is
to make people burst into peals of laughter.*

–Dinesh Verma

THE STRUGGLE BEGINS

Johnny Lever was inspired by Johny Walker to take up the career of a stand-up comedian. He had a passion for comedy and mimicry since he was a child and learnt his initial lessons of comedy in Yakutpura, Hyderabad where he spent his early childhood days. He followed comedians like Kishore Kumar and Mehmood in films and mimicry artist Dinesh Hingoo on stage.

He made up his mind to become a mimicry artist and approached Pratap Jani and Ram Kumar for guidance. They saw the dedication and talent in Johny and agreed to teach him the basics of mimicry.

"We are all gifted in some way or the other, and now I try to give back by advising and helping young, and upcoming comedians. This gift is not mine to keep. The more you give, the more you receive"

*We make a living by what we get; we
make a life by what we give.*

–Winston Churchill

Johnny was working with Hindustan Lever during the initial days of his career along with his father. In the factory, he used to entertain co-workers with his imitations of Elvis Presley. He performed at one of the factory functions on demand of his colleagues. He left the eyes of his co-workers and managers wide open with his fabulous performance. The union leader was so spellbound that he declared "from now on Johnny will be known as Johnny Lever".

He later on went on to perform for musical shows or the orchestras like Tabassum Hit Parade. After getting a bit of fame from there, he joined the group of legendary compositor Kalyan Ji – Anand Ji. As a part of the group, he attended many world tours and shows, in one such tour in 1982 he happened to be in the company of Amitabh Bachchan

"I started off as a labourer. The first time I went to work, a man ordered me to pick up the broom. I still remember his exact words. 'Since you're not well educated, you will have to do this work. After all, you're just carrying your father's legacy.' That was then and today, I stand before you as Johnny Lever - The Comedy King"

Hitting the milestone

Johny learnt a lot during his association with Kalyan Ji. He reveres Kalyan Ji still today as his mentor, a great philosopher and person filled with humor. While performing in such shows, his talent was noticed by actor, producer and director Sunil Dutt. He offered Johnny a role in his directorial, Dard Ka Rishta.

There was no looking back for this star who has till now spent days of great misery. He has earned a place for himself in the Bollywood as the Comedy King and there are scores of comedians and stand-up artists who regard Johnny as their inspiration. He has been nominated in the Filmfare Awards Best Comedian Category for 13 times and has bagged the offer thrice.

He is known for his philanthropic activities and for the large sums that he donates to the deprived and poor. A man with a golden heart, Johnny has always given a major share of his earnings for some noble cause and the best part is that he does it with silence.

> ***Charity should begin at home,***
> ***but should not stay there.***
>
> ***–Phillips Brooks***

Do you know?

A class 7th drop out, to support the family, Johnny sold pens on the street of Bombay.

It took him many years for making name in the industry but an undeterred Johnny kept on trying hard and finesse his skills.

> ***"Men are made stronger on realization***
> ***that the helping hand they need is at the***
> ***end of their arm".***

From living in India's biggest slum *'Dharavi'* to becoming India's most loved Bollywood comedian – Johnny has had a very interesting and inspiring journey. Lets recap his journey quickly in just a paragraph.

He was one among six siblings and his father worked at Hindustan Unilever (then Hindustan Lever Limited) and had to quit schooling due to financial hardships. He started working with his father at HUL but during free time, he used to entertain his colleagues by doing mimicry of Bollywood actors. In a function, he was asked to show his talent and he copied the talking style of some senior officials of HUL. After that he was given the nickname of Johnny Lever. He kept the name when he entered Bollywood. In 1981, he left the job of HUL after working for 6 years as he was not able to attend the office due to his shows. What's more, he was also earning good at that time. Rest as they say is all history.

For him, comedy is a serious business. He never takes his work for granted. In fact, he wanted to do some serious intense roles in Bollywood; but he knew that he is one comedian who can make people laugh without uttering a single word. How many times we start doing things and soon get into comfort zone. Getting into comfort zone means, no practice or less practice which leads to poor or very mediocre performance. Johnny has never taken any of his roles light, his daughter once revealed that though he is very foodie but he becomes cautious and stops eating rice and other junk food at least 2-3 days before he has any show.

If you are still looking for another lesson from Johnny – consider being grateful. He has deepest gratitude for all the odd jobs which he did before becoming a hero loved by so many. Be it selling pens or dancing in the streets of Mumbai or be it working at Hindustan Lever Limited for 6 years. In fact, HUL folks helped him find his strength of comedy and mimicry and as a gratitude symbol he has put Lever as his surname. Oh yes, he is a strong believer in the power of unseen hands God and prayers are part of his daily life.

So here we go with the two life lessons from Johnny Lever:

1. Never take your work for granted and be serious in preparation.

2. Be grateful to the people and to the almighty for all that you have.

* * *

Mithun Chakraborty

Don't give up and your dreams will come true.

Mithun Chakraborty was born on 16 June, 1950 in East Bengal, Pakistan(now in Bangladesh) in a Bengali family. He was named Gouranga Chakraborty by his parents. Winning National Award for the Best Actor for his debut movie itself, the name Mithun is synonymous of a milestone in Hindi Cinema.

*"During my struggling days I used to
dance at parties thinking that I would
get food to eat for at least that night"*

THE STRUGGLE BEGINS

Mithun made his acting debut in Mrinal Sen's directorial movie *Mrigaya* in 1976. Mithun left many head turned with his national award-winning performance in the film and went on to bag many offers for films. He created an immense fan  following for his classic dance moves. He is remembered particularly for his role of a street dancer as Jimmy in the 1982 film *Disco Dancer*. He got international fame especially in the erstwhile Soviet Union where he became a household name for his role in the film.

HITTING THE MILESTONE

Mithun after doing popular roles in movies like *Disco Dancer, Commando, Ghar Ek Mandir, Swarg Se Sundar, Pyar Jhukta Nahi, Watan Ke Rakhwale, Waqt ki Awaz, Swami Vivekanand, Agneepath, Jallad, Guru,Shapath, Gunahon Ka Devta, Pyar Ka Devta, Trinetra* and *Mere Sajana Saath Nibhana* started acting in his own productions. These movies that were shot in his Hotel in Ooty were all low-budget films. His role in Bengali film *Tahader Katha* (1992) earned him his 2nd National Award while got the third one for Hindi Film Swami Vivekananda that came in 1998,

He made a comeback to the mainstream Hindi cinema with Lucky, No Time for Love. Following which he has made appearances in movies like *Veer, Golmal 3, Housefull 2*, etc.

"Don't give up and your dreams will come true"

A graduate from the prestigious Scottish Church College of Kolkata, Mithun is also an alumnus of Film and Television Institute of India, Pune. He is one of the very few actors who could win a National Award for the debut film. He has made appearances in over 250 Hindi, Bengali, Oriya and Bhojpuri films. He turned an entrepreneur with the set up of his Monarch Group that is involved in the hospitality industry. He made his television debut as the judge for the reality shows Dance India Dance on the Zee TV.

DO YOU KNOW?

Mithun was a hardliner Naxalite involved in Bengal. He had left his home and the family for the movement. He returned home only after he lost his only brother to a tragic accident. He gave up the movement to support his family taking a big risk on his own life.

Remember your dreams and fight for them.
You must know what you want from life.
There is just one thing that makes your dream
become impossible: the fear of failure.

–Paulo Coelho

Mithun started acting for his own production because he wanted to work on his own terms. He even said no to a Mani Rathnam movie because he didn't want to experiment with his looks as he had many back to back movies of his own production lined up. He took a different turn from the league and started working for the B grade films produced under his own banner.

"Impossible is just a big word thrown around by small men who find it easier to live in the world they've been given than to explore the power they have to change it... Make it I AM POSSIBLE!!. Impossible is not a fact. It's an opinion! Impossible is not a declaration! It's a dare! Impossible is potential! Impossible is temporary! Impossible is nothing".

This guy, who is known as the *'Disco Dancer'* and he created marvels with his dancing skills, was once a Naxalite! Yes, you read it right.

His journey from Naxalite to Bollywood stardom is sheer inspiration and every time I sat to research about this star – all I explored about him gave me deep goose bumps.

Yet, here I would like to talk about a different side of this man – his benevolence for society. Less known are his acts of kindness yet these acts provide him deep satisfaction and strength to keep glowing. Did you know from his 4 children one is an adopted girl. Many years ago an infant child was found abandoned near a roadside garbage dump in West Bengal. When Mithun Da got to know about this he decided to rescue and adopt her. He adopted the infant girl from the NGO where she was kept after rescued. His wife Yogita Bali stood by him in this decision and they have brought her up as their own daughter. Dishani Chakraborty is now a grown up girl, pursued an acting course from he USA and has already made her debut in film industry with '*Holy Smoke* (2017)' and '*Underpass* (2018)'.

Because of his service to the society, especially the underprivileged – I consider him superhuman before a superhero. Let his good deeds inspire all of us to do the same in our own ways. We indeed owe a lot to the society and Mithun knows this so well.

Manoj Kumar

Manoj Kumar was born on 24 July 1937, in Abbottabad, North-West Frontier Province, British India as Harikishen Giri Goswami.

Manoj Kumar wanted to make Naya Bharat *with Rajesh Khanna in the lead. He also wanted to cast himself in a parallel role. The film never got made. Apparently Kumar and Khanna couldn't agree on whose name should appear first in the*

credit titles. During his superstardom Rajesh Khanna controlled every aspect of his projects, from director, to co-star, to music director. There was only one director who could control Khanna and that was Hrishikesh Mukherjee.

Don't get stuck in tiny things, think about the BIG impact your collaboration with some partners can create and let go the small things. When you let go the small things, you have the bandwidth to hold onto the big things. Don't get fussy about small things in life, people and your relationship with them can be more valuable than the ego over petty matters. ruled in the 1970s the nation drooled. Everyone wanted to work with the walking-talking-romancing hit machine. The mighty Gulzar came very close to working with the then-superstar Rajesh Khanna. The unknown story about the Gulzar-Khanna collaboration that never happened goes like this. Gulzar Saab and Khanna knew each other through the many films that Gulzar Saab wrote for Hrishikesh Mukherjee including Anand and Bawarchi. Gulzar Saab wanted to sign Rajesh Khanna for a romantic film which he had specially written for the Superstar. One night Rajesh Khanna called Gulzar home to his bungalow the famous Aashirwad. "Gulzar Saab who sleeps by 10 pm waited patiently till 1 am to meet the great man. But the Mighty Superstar continued drinking and cracking jokes with his durbar ignoring Gulzar Saab. He finally left in a huff, never to return again." Gulzar Saab signed Jeetendra for the same role the very next day. No matter how successful you are in your field, never ignore the people who can lift you even higher. Respect your well wishers and the people with whom you can always collaborate for bigger success.

* * *

www.ingramcontent.com/pod-product-compliance
Lightning Source LLC
LaVergne TN
LVHW020047160726
843469LV00043B/1536